THE SUFFERING
AND
THE GLORY

THE SUFFERING
AND
THE GLORY

David Prior

HODDER AND STOUGHTON
LONDON SYDNEY AUCKLAND TORONTO

British Library Cataloguing in Publication Data

Prior, David
    The suffering and the glory.
    1. Bible. N.T. Corinthians, 2nd   2. Suffering
    —Biblical teaching
    I. Title
    231'.8   BS2545.S9

    ISBN 0-340-38166-3

Hodder and Stoughton Editorial Office: 47 Bedford Square, London WC1B 3DP

For the people of God
past, present and future
of St Aldate's Church, Oxford:
with gratitude and expectancy

ACKNOWLEDGMENTS

I should like to thank two couples, whose great kindness enabled us to spend some time in their homes in the summer of 1984 – Tim and Clare Stunt, Ian and Elizabeth Aldred. This book was written in these two havens of peace and beauty. My special thanks again go to Betty Ho Sang for her immaculate and swift typing of the manuscript. It had some less efficient and less speedy treatment in journeys to and from the USA, but I trust it will be a positive contribution to the quest for authentic Christian discipleship, especially on both sides of the Atlantic.

CONTENTS

INTRODUCTION

About twenty years ago I was asked to write an article for one of the national Church newspapers. It was intended, I think, to show how my call to ordination had evolved and to explain what made me tick. I remember framing my remarks around St Paul's great statement of personal ambition – 'that I may know him and the power of his resurrection' (Phil. 3: 10). There is little I should want to change if I had to write a similar article today – but there is a lot I should have to add. Much of the additional material would, I trust, be a commentary on what Paul went on to say, but which I omitted: '. . . and may share his sufferings, becoming like him in his death.'

I am clear that my original half-quotation reflected my own background, both social and spiritual. Nearly a quarter of a century later we seem to be inundated with Christian teaching which not merely reflects, but effectively sanctions and proclaims such a dangerous half-truth. The so-called 'prosperity-churches' give such teaching a high profile, with their explicit promises of wealth, health and happiness for all those with 'real' faith.

But the glory-minus-suffering message is far more pervasively widespread than that. When I wrote the article in the mid 1960s, I could have been conveniently – and with reasonable accuracy – labelled a middle-class, evangelical, charismatic Englishman. In retrospect, all those epithets are significant. Each of the four contributed to my half-quoting St Paul. His emphasis on the glory *and* the suffering of being Christian did not sit comfortably alongside my need to achieve (one common characteristic of being 'middle-class'), my concern for visible results (endemic to evangelicalism), my search for something more lively, satisfying and impressive (which had been fed, though not created, by charismatic exposure), or my 'stiff upper lip' (which at least some Englishmen are taught to develop from childhood).

It seems plain to me now that a proper (by which word I mean a fully biblical) theology of suffering is essential, not simply for contemporary evangelical and charismatic Christianity in the West, but for the credibility of the gospel in a world which is suffering deeply, both in its present agony through famine, violence, oppression, unemployment and sickness, and in its foreboding of something even worse around the corner.

There is probably no part of the New Testament more relevant to this twin theme of suffering and glory than Paul's second letter to the Corinthians. If this letter was not extant and present in the New Testament, we should probably have formed a very inaccurate picture of Paul and of the gospel he proclaimed. From Luke's account in the Acts of the Apostles, as well as from virtually the rest of Paul's correspondence, the apostle comes across as a strong, self-contained and self-resourceful individualist, driven powerfully by the need to achieve and to succeed. His second letter to the Corinthians fills out, softens and humanises the man. He gradually becomes touchable and knowable. In a very important sense, the message he proclaimed also becomes consistently close to our own experience and aspirations – whereas without 2 Corinthians his experience and teaching can often leave us disillusioned, even depressed, because it seems only spasmodically to touch base with our daily routine.

Yet, in one sense, this is strange because Paul manifestly experienced suffering in ways which most of us can only conjure up in our imagination. On reflection, it seems to me that Paul comes closer to us in 2 Corinthians than elsewhere because he talks about and out of his failures, his weaknesses, his anxieties. He was intimately and inextricably linked in heart to the Christians in Corinth. This is clear from the text of both recorded letters. He got close enough to them to be vulnerable, so close that he was bound to get hurt.

The purpose of this book, therefore, is to explore the themes of suffering and glory from the various perspectives provided by Paul in 2 Corinthians. It is not a consecutive exposition of the text, although there is at times very serious study of key passages, phrases and even single keywords. It will become clear that a rich source-book for insight into the meaning of the text has been James Denney's commentary in the *Expositor's Bible*, published in 1894. This classic among bible commentaries has long been out of print. I have often searched for a copy in both obvious and unlikely places – always to no avail. Virtually every other volume in the series seems to be widely obtainable in second-hand bookshops, but not James Denney on 2 Corinthians.[1]

I borrowed a rare copy from Michael Green, with whom I often discussed the issues involved during five years of partnership and friendship in Christian ministry in Oxford, 1979–84. He has, of course, written his own book on Paul's correspondence with the Corinthians, *To Corinth with Love*,[2] but he would agree that his approach was different both in purpose and in content. I shall always be extremely grateful for the richness and the challenge of those five years.

However, 2 Corinthians is essentially a manifesto about the realities of Christian ministry. If this book has one purpose, it is to seek to provide a balanced and biblical perspective on what it means to be a Christian disciple, in particular to be a Christian minister. If at times it reads like an attack on certain approaches, if not individuals, I must express my sorrow in advance. My main reason for writing as I do is the growing number of disillusioned

Christians – disillusioned by a diet of teaching which has been unbalanced, short on realism and relevance, often lacking in integrity between what is taught and what is experienced (in both teacher and disciple), and holding out little hope, joy and love when people who are suffering become hungry for nourishment which they know, often only by instinct, must be available.

The first chapter deals with the general theme of suffering, as opened up by Paul at the outset of 2 Corinthians. The rest of the book branches out to cover many topics, often apparently unrelated to one another – but all of them touch on or arise out of the overall subject of suffering-and-glory, as being *together* the calling of the Christian in the world.

1

CREATIVE SUFFERING

'On Whit Sunday 1851 Florence Nightingale wrote: "My life is more difficult than almost any other kind. My life is more suffering than almost any other kind. Is it not God?"' In recording this, Elizabeth Longford comments, 'Whit Sunday had brought out in Florence the gift of tongues – and also the gift for almost limitless emotional exaggeration; it may be the gift of genius.'[1] Elizabeth Longford's assessment of what we would today call Florence Nightingale's charismatic experience on the Day of Pentecost, 1851, is almost as intriguing as Florence's own comments about suffering – 'Is it not God?' But we must resist the temptation to chase that hare.

Even after making due allowances for the mentality which sees God's will only in adversity and unpleasantness (everything pleasant being necessarily under suspicion), we can see the thrust of Florence Nightingale's comment on her personal suffering: 'Is it not God?' She is asserting that suffering is natural and normal to the Christian experience.

There is a growing trend to deny that. If you really allow God to work in you, it is often affirmed, you will be strong and successful, healthy and victorious. Conversely, if you suffer, show weakness or vulnerability, you are not being a proper Christian.

The day after writing this paragraph, I was sitting in a home in Switzerland with about a dozen others studying Psalm 77, in which personal anguish and a sense of alienation from God are uppermost in the first few verses. We had an honest and profitable time sharing our own similar experiences. After the natural end of the evening, an American pastor on a world trip spent twenty minutes explaining 'where I'm coming from and what I'm into'. He stressed his own strong conviction that the Church needs to realise that there is dynamite-power to be tapped, there is a life of victory to be experienced, there is healing and deliverance, there is release from depression, there is a far more glorious level of faith and reality than we have so far known in our generation. The secret? 'If we really fast and pray.'

The half-truths in these remarks are dangerous. Of course there is power and glory beyond our present experiences, but there is also suffering; not to mention such reality is lacking in integrity and sensitivity. The far more dangerous element in the pastor's remarks is the statement that the way into a more powerful and glorious experience of God is through our efforts in prayer and fasting. I hope that the rest of this book will explain why such an approach undermines the grace of God and, therefore, the path of Christian discipleship.

Even when this message is not explicitly proclaimed, it is tacitly communicated with almost equal clarity. Christians are often made to feel inadequate, if not complete failures, by this kind of message, spoken or silent. Sometimes the whole atmosphere or ethos in a local church breathes such a message. Many Christians feel they do not belong because they cannot match up to such expectations.

CULTURAL PRESSURE

It is important to understand a little more why such an

approach becomes so embedded. It is usually the result of social and cultural pressures. For example, many attitudes within Western evangelicalism owe more to a self-resourceful 'stand on your own feet' mentality than to the gospel of Jesus Christ. This has been aggravated by the influence, over the last sixty years or so, of an approach to Christian leadership which concentrates on those who are naturally gifted, educationally privileged, and socially attractive. More attention, time, energy and sheer money have been given to developing these people. There has also been a strong male emphasis in this tendency, often with a virtual denial of feelings, let alone weaknesses.

This combination of humanism, elitism and chauvinism has been often 'baptised' instead of rejected by Christians – with the result that an authentically biblical understanding of weakness and suffering has largely gone by default.

There is, in fact, another cultural factor in this common refusal to look properly at the reality of suffering, especially its inevitability. This comes from the influence of Eastern religions, not least the Western popularisations of Hinduism in the last twenty or thirty years. One of the essential tenets of this philosophy is that the reality of God within a person is to be discovered through an interior journey away from the harsh realities of the world. Such escapism is a popular way of dealing – or rather, *not* dealing – with suffering and hardship. Sadly, much contemporary Christian spirituality is of this pietistic nature. Praise and prayer become pain-killers instead of a road into the heart of God.

At bottom, whether Western or Eastern in origin, our unwillingness realistically to face the pain, suffering, failure and weakness all around us and within us is nothing more than a fairly flabby capitulation to our lower nature. This is why Paul's perspectives in 2 Corinthians on his own sufferings are so penetrating. He takes us out of introversion, escapism and unbelief into a robust appreciation of the creative purposes of God in what is happening to us. At the outset of his letter, he gives us five perspectives.

1. God shares our suffering. A few months ago I had a visit in Oxford from an Indian evangelist, called Azariah, whom I had not seen since we were at theological college together in Cambridge about eighteen years ago. His life has been full of great adversity and suffering. For about an hour we shared much of what had happened since we last met. Then we prayed. Azariah started immediately with the following simple, but profound, prayer, 'Father, thank you that you have been with us in all that we have been through.'

That, essentially Christian, statement is at the heart of Paul's expression of praise at the beginning of his letter: 'Blessed be the God and Father of our Lord Jesus Christ, the Father of mercies and God of all comfort, who comforts us in all our affliction' (2 Cor. 1: 3-4). In effect, Paul is here affirming that he has come to know God in his sufferings in a way he never knew him before - i.e. as Father, the Father of mercies. Not only had he known the presence of God in his sufferings; he had penetrated more into the very nature of God, not merely in an intellectual way, but in personal experience.

When we are going through the mill in any way, it lays bare what our picture of God is really like. We so often see suffering as alien; we think that God has forgotten us or failed us. It seems as if he has put his knife into us. We can then allow God to become to us anything but 'the Father of mercies and the God of all comfort'. An important clue to Paul's own experience is given in his earlier phrase, 'the God and Father of our Lord Jesus Christ'. In this phrase he is calling our attention to the way God the Father related to his Son, Jesus, especially in the intensity of his sufferings. Even in the white heat of his passion, Jesus was still calling God, 'Abba, Father' (Luke 22: 42; 23: 34).

JESUS ON THE CROSS

On the cross, Jesus did actually experience being forsaken by the Father (Matt. 27: 46), as he endured suffering which we (as a direct consequence) need never face. The first implication for us of that experience by Jesus is that, however deeply we suffer, we are *not* forsaken by the Father. He is right there with us in our suffering to reveal himself as our Father. It is precisely in his own nature thus to respond to his children when they suffer – he cannot do otherwise: 'God delivers the afflicted, not because he is under any obligation to do so, but out of sheer mercy.'[2]

When, therefore, we turn to God in prayer in our suffering, we are going to the very heart of God and flinging ourselves on his mercy. This is an important perspective, because we can easily become side-tracked into thinking that what causes God to act is the fervour or the faith of our prayers. The solid ground for our praying is not anything we drum up, but the unchanging nature of God as our Father, the Father of mercies. This is substantiated by the root-meaning of 'comfort', which indicates someone called in to stand alongside (the same word used of the Holy Spirit as our 'Comforter' or 'Paraclete'). The Lord stands alongside us in our sufferings to reveal himself more and more as our Father.

The basic meanings of the two words translated 'affliction' and 'sufferings' in this opening part of 2 Corinthians both speak of what happens to us without any choice or action on our part. The first word means 'pressure', and is used by Jesus in his farewell exhortation to his disciples: 'In the world you have tribulation; but be of good cheer, I have overcome the world' (John 16: 33). That kind of pressure is inevitable. The other word has the connotation of what others force upon us. That, also, is inevitable. Paul's experience of suffering, as outlined in these verses, describes any parallel situation in which we ourselves are on the receiving end of treatment or circumstances which we would not choose for ourselves. In such a situation God comes in as Father and stands alongside, as he did with Paul and as he did with Jesus. God shares our sufferings. He is there within them so that he can reveal more of himself to us. If we make this our prayer and our determination, we shall not be disappointed.

2. *We share Christ's sufferings.* It needs to be said immediately that there is a fundamental way in which we cannot share in Christ's sufferings – i.e. we cannot, by our suffering, atone for our own or for anyone else's, sins. Only the atoning power of Christ's death on the cross can do that – there are no 'lesser Calvaries', as one of the 'national' hymns would have us sing:

> Still stands his Cross from that dread hour to this,
> Like some bright star above the dark abyss;
> Still, through the veil, the Victor's pitying eyes,
> Look down to bless our lesser Calvaries.[3]

The hymn is unacceptable because it attempts to attach our sufferings – in that case in war – to the sufferings of Christ. Paul is concerned, rather, to explain how Christ's sufferings continue in the sufferings of his people. In another passage Paul asserts, 'in my flesh I complete what is lacking in Christ's afflictions for the sake of his body, that is, the church' (Col. 1: 24). So here, in 2 Corinthians, Paul writes: 'The sufferings of Christ abound in us' (1: 5 AV). Jesus is *still* suffering.

I believe this aspect of sharing Christ's sufferings does not refer only to specific persecution for the sake of Christ. It has a wider application than that. If we choose to make ourselves available to one another in the body of Christ, it will mean daily dying and suffering – dying to ourselves and carrying the sufferings of others in our feelings and personality. This is particularly true of intercessory prayer – as Paul makes plain later: 'We are afflicted in every way,

but not crushed ... always carrying in the body the death
of Jesus, so that the life of Jesus may also be manifested in
our bodies. For while we live we are always being given up
to death for Jesus' sake, so that the life of Jesus may be
manifested in our mortal flesh. So death is at work in us,
but life in you' (2 Cor. 4: 8–12).

LOVE WHICH SUFFERS

Solidarity is at the heart of such ministry. Paul is saying
that, if there is going to be spiritual life anywhere for
anyone, someone somewhere has got to suffer. This
perspective on the relatively innocuous statement, 'If one
member suffers, all suffer together' (1 Cor. 12: 26), strongly
challenges our lack of commitment to one another in the
body of Christ, as well as our self-indulgent refusal to face
– or at least hesitancy about – suffering as Christians. As
we walk the way of Christ, who still suffers and grieves for
his Church and his world because of his immense love for
us, we shall know suffering. That kind of suffering goes
deep into our very being and personhood; we are
profoundly affected by it – and this, presumably, is why we
instinctively draw away from it and often choose not to
walk that road.

We must, however, face up realistically to the implications of such widespread rejection today of suffering as
authentically Christian. The unavoidable implication of
Paul's teaching is that spiritual life is prevented to the
extent that the Church is not prepared to embrace this
kind of suffering. In other words, whenever I flinch from,
let alone refuse to follow, the path of personal suffering –
expressed either in intercession or in evangelism or in
practical holiness or in prophetic witness – I am denying
spiritual life to others elsewhere.

A parable of this truth seems to be vividly presented in
much healing ministry, when the person God is using as

his instrument will often feel physically the pain of the sufferer in the same part of his own body, as a prelude to the Lord's healing being ministered.

Examples of this same truth are, unfortunately, virtually impossible to substantiate – by its very nature it is an invisible and intangible truth. We are sometimes given clues: for example, when I was in Uganda in 1981, I was powerfully struck and humbled by the intercessory burden carried for the Church in Britain by the greatly-suffering Church in Uganda. There is remarkable spiritual life in many parts of the Ugandan Church, and I found myself wondering whether re-emerging life in the Church in Britain is not due to such intercession by those who have – for more than a decade – been learning so painfully how to embrace unrelieved and inexplicable suffering. In a very real sense, death is at work in them and that means life for us.

Indeed, when the books that matter are opened, I have a suspicion that the significant rewards will be for those who have borne the heat and burden of the day in such deliberately-chosen identification with Jesus in his own permanent work of intercession.[4] Notable among such Christians will surely be those in virtually every congregation or community who quietly continue constant in prayer, usually without anyone knowing except God. It is a costly ministry, and one to which Paul urgently summons the Corinthians: 'You also must help us by prayer' (2 Cor. 1: 11).

James Denney provides a perceptive commentary on the whole subject of sharing Christ's sufferings.

Christ suffered alone; there is ... a solitary, incommunicable greatness in his Cross. Even when Christ's sufferings come upon us, there is a difference ... We do from gratitude what he did from pure love. We suffer in his company, sustained by his comfort; he suffered uncomforted and unsustained.[5]

3. *Others share our suffering.* Such a sentence is virtually a truism – until we are going through the mill. One of the ways suffering reaches and affects us is in impairing our judgment. Our assessment of the facts becomes inaccurate. This happens in one particular way: we genuinely feel that nobody knows the trouble we know, that we are alone in our pain and anguish. We then clam up and often find it very difficult to share what we are going through.

Such a situation Satan delights to exploit to his own advantage, chiefly by locking us up in introspection and confirming our suspicions that we are unique in our suffering. Paul, however, states simply that 'you... endure the same sufferings that we suffer' (2 Cor. 1: 6). What was true for Paul and the Christians at Corinth in their particular situation is generally true for Christians anywhere. The trouble comes because some of us are more adept and determined in concealing the way we are feeling.

The chief reason why this needs to be tackled is that our frequent unwillingness to share our weaknesses, as pinpointed by the things we have to suffer, is a serious obstacle to true fellowship. It is rarely recognised, let alone acted upon, that we meet one another as real people when we are freed to share where we are hurting and failing. Time and time again we discovered this in our staff-team both in Oxford and Cape Town. It is extremely easy for full-time ministers, in particular, to share the blessings God is bringing and the results we are seeing. It is usually more difficult to share where it is hard and impossible. The competitive spirit dies with difficulty. Once we were able, in our staff meetings, to recognise and resist this powerful force, and instead to be honest and open with one another, we began to experience the fellowship of the Holy Spirit in very new ways. Countless Christians have discovered the same truth in house meetings, and in other situations.

It is unlikely that we shall open up, when in pain or

under pressure, except to people with whom we are already feeling at home. The isolated Christian is doubly prone to introspection and its fruit. When someone shares what he is going through, at least two things happen immediately: somebody else – and often several others – is given the freedom to share his own problems and needs; and the original sharer discovers he is not alone in his suffering.

FACING REALITY

One of the pernicious results of teaching which leads Christians to expect buoyancy and victory as the normative results of 'real faith' is a refusal to face up to the presence of affliction and the experience of weakness or failure. Many Christians actually refuse to face reality and enter the twilight world of a spiritual schizophrenic, unable to discern the real from the imaginary. A classic example of this approach comes when a sick person, having been prayed for, is told that he is no longer sick, even when he manifestly is. Faith is presented, in such circumstances, as believing what is not true, instead of resting in the love and power of a Father-God who never changes.

Such a sufferer ends up almost compelled to deny that he is suffering, certainly in the company of those who have ministered to him. When fellowship depends upon the amount of faith we can muster, particularly when we are in adversity, we have perverted the gift of God to his people. 'Welcome one another, therefore, as Christ has welcomed you' (Rom. 15: 7) is Paul's exhortation elsewhere, reminding us that God accepts us as we are and by his Spirit enables us to accept one another as we are. Any conspiracy of competence, victory or buoyancy reinforces the scheming of Satan in the life of the Church: those who think they have it all together are encouraged in their self-delusion; those who know they haven't keep quiet. The next step for the former is a big crash; the next step for the latter is to distance themselves from the life of that particular Church – and often from Christian fellowship altogether.

4. *We share God's comfort with those who are suffering.* A situation where suffering is denied or covered over also prevents God's ministry of mutual support and encouragement, a ministry which lies at the heart of Paul's opening remarks to the Corinthians. Put simply, if I do not admit I am suffering, nobody can come alongside me with God's comfort. We are, as Christians, called into this mutual ministry, by virtue of being members together of the body of Christ. The rhythm of suffering and comfort is not accidental: it is God's specific purpose and intention. As Denney writes, 'Some mysteries would be cleared up if we had love enough to see the ties by which our life is indissolubly linked to others.'[6]

This divine purpose is underlined by the phrase 'so that . . .' in chapter one, verse four, of 2 Corinthians, where Paul is firm in asserting that God 'comforts us in all our affliction, so that we may be able to comfort those who are in any affliction, with the comfort with which we ourselves are comforted by God.' God comes alongside us in our troubles because he wants us to come alongside others in their troubles. This illustrates a fundamental fact of Christian discipleship: we lose what we try to keep; we gain what we give away.[7]

When, therefore, the Lord gives us his encouragement and strength in our affliction, we should immediately be on the lookout for others around us who need similar help. This does not often happen: we remain uncertain and introspective, perhaps not wanting to assume too readily that we truly have received God's strength. It seems to me that the best way to preserve our blessings is immediately to share them. Naturally this requires sensitivity and compassion, but most of us need to be more ready to give away what we have received from the Lord. Whatever God gives us is for passing on.

There may well be a hint, in these particular words of Paul, of a further biblical perspective on suffering – i.e. God actually brings us into the furnace of affliction with the express purpose of refining us as individuals and binding us to one another in his family. The whole issue of God's active will and God's permissive will (or what he directly sends and what he allows to happen) has been the subject of immense theological and philosophical debate over the centuries. It is, naturally, impossible to conclude it in a paragraph; but it might well be time to reinstate the more direct vocabulary of the Bible, instead of overlaying or re-interpreting it in contemporary (and often outworn) language.

THE EXAMPLE OF JOB

For example, the book of Job contains statements about God's activity in his world which are far more bold than our current terminology. Job's initial reaction to his repeated troubles was, 'the Lord gave, and the Lord has taken away; blessed be the name of the Lord' (1: 21). A bit later, in reaction to his wife's anti-faith, Job declares: 'Shall we receive good at the hand of God, and shall we not receive evil?' (2: 10). We expect Job's comforters to come out with pious platitudes, but Eliphaz's words bear patient pondering: 'despise not the chastening of the Almighty. For he wounds, but he binds up; he smites, but his hands heal' (5: 17–18). This friend's advice was not so much untrue as untimely. At the right moment Job was actually able to receive the truth in what Eliphaz had said earlier, but only as the result of a clearer and more intimate experience of God.

There are other parts of the Old Testament which speak with equal pungency: '"See now that I, even I, am he, and there is no god beside me; I kill and I make alive; I wound and I heal...'" (Deut. 32: 39). 'The Lord kills and brings to life; he brings down to Sheol and raises up' (1 Sam. 2: 6). 'Come, let us return to the Lord; for he has torn, that he may heal us; he has stricken, and he will bind us up' (Hos. 6: 1). Isaiah refers to 'the day when the Lord binds up the hurt of his people, and heals the wounds inflicted by his blow' (Isa. 30: 26).

Whatever role is permitted to Satan, in the book of Job in particular, the enemy's activity is consistently seen as part of the purposes of God, in that he weaves it all into his overall design. We are constantly in danger of developing a dualistic approach, which attributes certain (normally the negative and the unpleasant) experiences to Satan, and other situations to God and his blessing. The God revealed in the Bible, the God and Father of our Lord Jesus Christ, 'accomplishes *all* things according to the counsel of his will' (Eph. 1: 11), and is continuously at work 'for good' (Rom. 8: 28) in *everything* that happens.

The trouble comes when, believing this in our heads, we are lured away from its stabilising power when we are in the midst of suffering. We then tend to give Satan far more credit and leeway than he deserves, and equally we find it hard to trace the footprints of our Father God in the storm. At such times a positive discipline would be to say to ourselves: 'God is my Father; he loves me; he knows what I am going through; he knows what he is doing; this is all part of his purpose for me; he has sent/done this to enable me to know him better and to know my fellow-Christians better; and he wants me to share what I am learning with others.'

In this way, we shall be better disposed to embrace the consistent thrust of the New Testament when it says, for example, 'Count it all joy, my brethren, when you meet various trials, for you know that the testing of your faith produces steadfastness' (Jas. 1: 2-3), or 'now for a little while you may have to suffer various trials, so that the genuineness of your faith, more precious than gold which though perishable is tested by fire, may redound to praise and glory and honour at the revelation of Jesus Christ' (1 Pet. 1: 6-7).

REBELLIOUS GOLD

The express purpose of God, therefore, in our sufferings is our personal wholeness and the wholeness of his body, the Church. The two are inextricably linked. Our root problem, according to the word of God, is rebelliousness – wanting to have things our own way, and to go our own way independently of one another. It is at this rebelliousness which the Lord is irrevocably chipping away, and one of his prime instruments is fire – the metaphor Peter uses in the passage just quoted.

A few years ago I was reading the house magazine of the vast South African mining conglomerate, Anglo-American. One particular article was describing recent advances in the discovery, mining and use of gold. Modern technology has apparently made it possible to make commercial use of over 90 per cent of the ore recovered from the ground. Special research is being pursued to see what can be done with the remaining 8 or 9 per cent. Scientists have a phrase for this last percentage – they call it 'rebellious gold'.

We are God's rebellious gold – rebellious through and through, not just a small percentage of our character and personality. He puts us through the furnace of suffering to get rid of the dross and to refine us. He is stamping in us the pattern of his Son, Jesus. For a pattern to become permanently fixed in china, it has to be burned in. In our sufferings God our Father is burning into us the character of Jesus. Those who are enabled to accept this work of God's grace become crucial and creative catalysts for God's work in the lives of other believers: 'Are they not among

God's best gifts to his church, those whom he has qualified to console by consoling them in the fire?'[8]

5. *Our sufferings sharpen our reliance on God.* In verses 8–11 of chapter 1, Paul is more explicit about his own sufferings. Scholars are uncertain about which particular occasion he means by 'the affliction we experienced in Asia'. It is more than possible that he is describing his inner turmoil during the harrowing events at Ephesus, the capital city of the Roman province of Asia Minor, narrated by Luke in Acts 19. In his first letter to the Corinthians Paul refers to the time when 'I fought with wild beasts at Ephesus' (1 Cor. 15: 32). When we look more closely at what happened to Paul at Ephesus during those initial two years or more, the reasons for Paul's exhaustion and anguish become more apparent.

For example, Ephesus was a centre of occult practices. It was not long before the preaching of the gospel provoked considerable opposition. Evil spirits came out of many people. A dramatic incident ensued involving the seven sons of a Jewish high priest called Sceva. These brothers travelled around exorcising any willing patients and, when Paul came to town, they 'undertook to pronounce the name of the Lord Jesus over those who had evil spirits, saying, "I adjure you by the Jesus whom Paul preaches"' (Acts 19: 13). This talismanic, magical use of the name of Jesus (without any submission of their lives to Jesus as Lord) predictably caused havoc – and also led to a stepping-up of direct ministry to people who needed to renounce different kinds of superstitions and occult practices. This direct encounter with occult forces always takes its toll on Christians involved in such ministry: one of the chief results is sheer exhaustion, usually out of all proportion to the time and energy expended. Paul would have been spiritually and physically vulnerable.

VESTED INTERESTS

His next exposure at Ephesus was to the extremely powerful vested interests in the commercial and business circles of the city. As the word of God made headway among the Ephesians, they began to give up their worship of the local goddess, Artemis or Diana. This cult produced silver shrines of the goddess, which were the prized possession of her devotees. The local shop-steward of the national union of silversmiths, a man named Demetrius, called a special meeting to stress the seriousness of this 'apostasy' for 'this trade of ours' (Acts 19: 27). He added a few timely, rabble-rousing remarks about the threat to the honour and magnificence of 'the great goddess Artemis'. When people's wealth, let alone very livelihood, is under threat, unholy forces go to work in self-defence. Paul and his companions became the target for this rage and bitterness. Similar situations today make plain how taxing, if not draining, it is to be on the receiving-end of such treatment.

Paul's next encounter with 'wild beasts' at Ephesus was in the mob violence which was provoked by the wrath of the silversmiths. Two of his friends, Gaius and Aristarchus, were about to be lynched by the angry crowd in the local open-air theatre, and Paul was understandably raring to go in among the mob to rescue them. He was restrained only with great difficulty from such a dangerous move in such a volatile situation. The crowd filling the stadium chanted the name of Artemis for two solid hours, while Paul and his friends looked on helplessly. Eventually, the situation was recovered by the town clerk (of all people) and Alexander, another of the local authority-figures. Mob violence is a frightening thing to see, let alone to provoke by one's own behaviour. On top of opposition from occult forces and economic vested interests, this pressure surely took its toll of Paul.

Apart from these three extraordinary experiences, Paul

was involved in a daily schedule at Ephesus which would have built up its own pressure on him. In a sub-tropical climate which would have been enervating anyway, Paul taught his way daily through the searing heat of the siesta period (i.e. 11 a.m. to 3 p.m.) in the hall of Tyrannus. This was not simply straight teaching, but majored on the cut-and-thrust of public debate. If that was not sufficiently exhausting, he worked for a living for the rest of each day[9] in his trade of tent-making, probably from 7 to 11 in the morning, and from 3 to 7 in the late afternoon.

In others, Paul pushed himself – and was pushed – extremely hard during those two to three years in Ephesus. The pace of his daily routine, the intensity of his temperament and of his preaching God's word, the sheer hard work which he devoted to pastoral care of the young Church,[10] the distinctively savage opposition he received – these and other factors must have left him exhausted, vulnerable and in desperate need of both rest and the renewing touch of God. At the climax of these events in Ephesus, his adrenalin was flowing fast[11] – it would not be at all surprising if, like Elijah after the events on Mount Carmel (1 Kgs. 18 and 19), he suffered a violent reaction by way of a depression such as he describes to his friends at Corinth, 'we were so utterly, unbearably crushed that we despaired of life itself. Why, we felt that we had received the sentence of death' (2 Cor. 1: 8–9).

PAUL'S DEPRESSION

I believe it is not exaggerating these events and words to say that Paul was in acute reactive depression. He was prepared to call it a day: life was not worth living, because it was so pressurised. I have taken time to describe a very likely background to Paul's description of his feelings in Asia, because the ingredients of his own experience are not unusual for any Christian today who is taking his calling seriously. Some of the pressures Paul – like us – brought upon himself; others were the direct results of his becoming the target for those who did not like him or (more particularly) his message and its implications. Many Christians today are living daily at the kind of pace which inevitably intensifies the pressures which invariably beat down on loyal disciples of Jesus. Even though this combination of a frantic daily routine and virulent opposition is taking an increasing toll on our family and own inner resources, we fail to hear what God is saying to us.

The obvious word from God would be 'Calm down', and that may well turn out to be the ultimate message which he is trying to get through to us. For Paul it was a rather different – and more searching – message: 'Stop relying on your own energies, experience and efforts; start relying on me.' That is a far more searching instruction, because simply taking a break or slowing the pace does not necessarily get to the heart of the problem. In Asia Minor, Paul was brought into a situation where he could not cope, where he failed, where his own weaknesses were exposed. He had faced many challenging situations before, but here he was at the end of his tether. God deliberately brings us to such situations, into impossible circumstances to which we have no answer, and to which there is no human answer. He forces us to taste our inadequacy, our failure.

In such hopeless, helpless situations we are compelled, like Paul, to depend on the Lord, not on ourselves. If the result of going through the mill is that kind of deepened trust in God and experience of his power to deliver, then will we not choose to embrace the suffering? Such is God's love for us and, because of that love, such is his solid determination to make us like Jesus, that he will probably push us in the deep end if we are not prepared to jump in ourselves. If we will not get in the deep end, we shall not learn to swim.

Our sufferings sharpen our reliance on God, and a deepening reliance on God opens for us the gateway to experiencing more of the glory of God. 'There is a point at which the invisible world and its glories... become visible, real and inspiring to men. It is the point at which we suffer with Christ's sufferings.'[12]

* * *

This, then, is the theme of 2 Corinthians, as summarised in the first few verses of chapter one. The rest of Paul's letter flows out of and illustrates this great theme from many different angles. 'The church at Corinth thought it could by-pass affliction on the way to comfort. The theme of this epistle is that this is impossible. Christian discipline means... a progressive weakening of man's instinctive self-confidence, and of the self-despair to which this leads, and the growth of radical confidence in God.'[13]

2

INTEGRITY

When Christians are unable, for whatever reason, to face honestly the call to suffering and the reality of personal weakness and failure, one of the earliest and most serious casualties is integrity. This evocative word describes an inner consistency which is demonstrated by a straightforward reliability in what a person says and does. If someone is convinced that a Christian ought to experience and demonstrate continuous victory – and that anything less indicates failure and faithlessness – a frightening amount of cover-up, make-believe and self-condemnation is inevitable.

The more a person goes on public record as expecting a high level of achievement and success, the more difficult it becomes to retract such expectations and to face reality. Christian success stories often reflect this fact: the problems and the failures have been so constantly glossed over in frequent narration of all that has happened, that they actually leave the conscious memory of the leading actors in the drama. A mentality is thus gradually formed which never faces up to failure and non-achievement because it does not want to. It does not want to face up to these things because it cannot afford to do so – if it is going to survive: and survive, of course, it must because of all that is involved if it doesn't.

It is, therefore, all the more striking that Paul's own boast to the Corinthians concerns the consistent integrity of his daily behaviour. In 1: 12–13 immediately following the description of his personal suffering in Asia Minor, he declares: 'For our boast is this, the testimony of our conscience that we have behaved in the world, and still more toward you, with straightforwardness[1] and godly sincerity, not by earthly wisdom but by the grace of God.'

Because the theme of boasting becomes so uppermost in Paul's mind towards the end of the letter,[2] it is very significant that he speaks so plainly of his integrity as a matter for personal pride. Paul hated boasting about his own achievements or experience; this boast is unsolicited and lays bare what he regarded to be of fundamental importance for Christian discipleship and ministry. If we lack such integrity, our witness is seriously impaired.

COMPLETE CONSISTENCY

Paul claims that he always acts straightforwardly and openly, whether the audience is the world at large or the church at Corinth. He is not one man with unbelievers and another with Christians. He is not a different person at home from the person he is away from home. He does not behave in one way when in Corinth and another way in, say, Ephesus or Jerusalem. In particular, he is not given to writing one thing in his letters and saying the opposite face to face (which his detractors at Corinth rather laboured[3]).

Paul's commitment to such integrity stands out in sheer contrast to the recently-publicised attitude of one of today's leading thinkers, A. J. Ayer, for twenty years Wykeham Professor of Logic at Oxford. I can recall, with some clarity and regret, the way Professor Ayer's influence affected me when I was studying philosophy at Oxford in the early 1960s. He developed a strong emphasis on linguistic analysis, with its insistence on the meaning of words in expressing ideas rather than on discovering ethical foundations and values for daily living. My own grounding in Christian truth in those days was not sure enough for me to engage with such philosophical theory in explicitly Christian terms. I chose, therefore, to keep my life in two compartments – my studies and my faith.

Imagine, then, my fascination the other day to read these comments by Professor Ayer in reflecting on his life: 'If you are writing philosophy, it seems to me that the important thing is to be exact and lucid, and on the whole to avoid ornamentation. But there's no reason why that should spill over into the rest of one's life ... When I'm not actually working, I want to leave my work behind me. I do, perhaps, like to keep things in compartments.'[4]

For Paul, by contrast, integrity was a matter of 'conscience'. He would have been unable to live with himself if he was aware of any basic non-integrity in his life. Paul's insistence on this inner cleanness was clearly a constant priority. When on trial before the Sanhedrin in Jerusalem, he began his defence with these words: 'I have lived before God in all good conscience up to this day' (Acts 23: 1). He repeated the affirmation when brought before the Roman governor, Felix: 'I always take pains to have a clear conscience toward God and toward men' (Acts 24: 16). To Felix he explained carefully that this priority of a clear conscience was ingrained into him by his certain conviction about a coming time of judgment before God: 'I worship the God of our fathers ... having a hope in God ... that there will be a resurrection of both the just and the unjust' (Acts 24: 14-15).

Paul's integrity, therefore, was a matter of conscience, because he knew he would have to answer to God for his behaviour, 'we make it our aim to please him. For we must all appear before the judgment seat of Christ, so that each one may receive good or evil, according to what he has done in the body' (2 Cor. 5: 9-10). It is very easy, when heavily involved in Christian ministry (especially when it has been given a high profile), to forget this basic fact. Paul did not forget it.

What does he mean by the phrase 'with straightforwardness and godly sincerity'? Of what does integrity consist? How do we come by it and grow in it? The first Greek word stresses letting the sun of God's love and truth shine into our motives and inner being. Paul uses it again at 2: 17 to describe the way he handles God's word – an aspect of Christian ministry we shall examine later. He uses it also in 1 Corinthians, chapter 5, verse 8, when urging the church at Corinth to purge out 'the leaven of malice and evil' from its community life, and to worship God 'with the unleavened bread of sincerity/straightforwardness and truth'. The particular context has been dealing with a notorious Corinthian situation, in which they were condoning, even applauding, blatant sexual immorality in the fellowship. Such inconsistency must be faced up to in the light of God's holy demands and summarily dealt with, states the apostle.

The first essential ingredient of Paul's integrity, therefore, was a consistent openness in letting God's truth expose everything unworthy and false. He did not justify such things in himself or in others. He dealt with them as a matter of urgency, both for the health of the Church and for the freedom of his own conscience against meeting his Lord face to face.

LACK OF COMPLEXITY

The second Greek word stresses lack of complexity. Paul uses the same word on four other occasions in this same letter: three times in connection with generous giving to others in need (2 Cor. 8: 2–3; 9: 11, 13), and once to describe the Corinthians' personal relationship with the Lord Jesus Christ (2: 17). Both our giving to God and our love for God can become laden with complexity. In my own experience such loss of straightforwardness and simplicity has been caused by my own movement away from a childlike trust in God as my Father. Instead of taking this relationship on trust, as given and sustained by the power of the Holy Spirit, I can easily begin to examine its dynamics, question its sincerity, doubt its very existence.

A child does not behave like that with its father. The relationship is accepted without questioning. If the child needs something, wants something, feels something, sees something, receives something, he naturally shares his heart with his father. Very often, the same straight-forwardness will be shown to others who come into contact with the child. There is a spontaneous, unaffected directness in the way a child relates to his father and to everyone else. Of course, it seems to become complicated and spoiled all too soon, but it is surely this straight-forward trust and openness which Jesus himself stressed when saying: 'Truly, I say to you, unless you turn and become like children, you will never enter the kingdom of heaven' (Matt. 18: 3).

When Paul, then, refers to his straightforwardness – in general behaviour, but particularly with the Corinthians – he seems to be referring to the direct way in which he relates to people, springing out of the open, uncomplicated way in which he relates to the Lord. An important implication of this for Paul is explained later, when he insists that he does not want anyone to 'think more of me than he sees in me or hears from me' (2 Cor. 12: 6). Here, in the first chapter, he applies this priority specifically to his letter-writing, 'we write to you nothing but what you can read and understand' (1: 13), his way of saying, 'I mean what I say and I say what I mean'. Again, he places this integrity in the context of his answerability to God, because he at once calls attention to 'the day of the Lord Jesus' (1: 14).

Elsewhere, Paul makes it plain that such integrity is not

a natural quality, nor is it possessed once and for all – we are to grow into it: 'And it is my prayer that your love may abound more and more, with knowledge and all discernment, so that you may approve what is excellent, and may be pure [sincere] and blameless for the day of Jesus Christ' (Phil. 1: 9-11).

THE GRACE OF GOD

Nevertheless, such transparency and straightforwardness are possible 'not by earthly wisdom but by the grace of God' (2 Cor. 1: 12-13). This contrast underlines that only God can produce this integrity. Paul boasts of it precisely because God has done it by his grace, and therefore the glory is his alone. Paul has not made himself a man of integrity by his own willpower or moral effort (the force of the phrase 'earthly wisdom').

It is important to be clear about the nature of this integrity and the way we develop it. Some Christians seem to think that everybody is necessarily complex, that there are always hidden motives in what a person does, and that there is in every individual's personality a subterranean minefield which requires careful negotiation and skilled handling. No doubt many people are like that, but many are not. If our aim is integrity – not achievement – if we are enabled by God's grace to stand firm in our relationship to him as Father and allow his light to shine into our inner hearts, if we keep 'the day of Jesus Christ' in front of our eyes as a healthy and salutary reminder of where we are heading – then there will gradually develop a straightforward, reliable character which reflects the character of God himself.

This is the force of Paul's remarks later in chapter one about the promises of God finding their 'Yes' in Jesus. Paul was being accused of being completely unreliable. His detractors at Corinth seem to have been making a mountain out of a molehill. He had hoped to visit them all at Corinth on his missionary travels, and had let them know of his intentions accordingly. There had been a necessary element of uncertainty in his plans, which certain people had chosen to interpret as vacillation and unreliability: Paul, they claimed, was acting 'according to the flesh', and you could rely on his plans no more than any other worldly man. He said one thing, and did the opposite. His 'Yes' might well turn out to be 'No'. He was not a man of his word.

GOD'S RELIABILITY

So the picture was built up of a Christian lacking basic integrity. It is instructive to see that Paul bases his defence, not so much in what he did or did not promise, but in the character of God as revealed in Jesus.[5] Paul's commitment to Jesus as his Lord genuinely included taking Jesus as his model, not merely in outward behaviour but in essential attitudes. God has been completely straightforward and reliable with us – and the career of Jesus demonstrated it fully and finally – and this leaves Christians with an obligation to be similarly straightforward and reliable.

In Jesus God has said, and continues to say, 'Yes' to us. Everything he has ever promised us he has made good in Jesus. Has God offered to forgive our sins? We have forgiveness in Jesus. Has God promised never to fail us or forsake us? We have the presence of God with us in Jesus to the end of time. Has God promised to put a new heart and a new spirit within us? Through Jesus we have the gift of the Holy Spirit. Has God promised to call us his own sons and daughters, to guide us and to provide for us? We are children of God in his Son, Jesus, and this God will be our guide for ever. Has God promised us eternal life and an inheritance in heaven? These gifts are ours in Jesus. 'God has never put a hope or a prayer into man's heart that is not answered and satisfied abundantly in his Son.'[6]

In every way, therefore, God has demonstrated his positive commitment to us in Jesus: 'For all the promises of God find their Yes in him' (2 Cor. 1: 20). More than that, 'But it is God who establishes us with you in Christ and has commissioned us; he has put his seal upon us and given us his Spirit in our hearts as a guarantee' (2 Cor. 1: 21-2). The four key words in this sentence all illustrate the positive and affirmative attitude which God has taken towards us – establish, commission, seal, guarantee. All the unchangeable character of God the Holy Trinity lies behind this grace in salvation. God has said an irrevocable 'Yes' to us. 'Amen is all that God leaves for us to say ... God's glory is identified with the recognition and appropriation by men of his goodness and faithfulness in Jesus Christ.'[7]

Such an attitude should be the feature of any Christian's behaviour, especially in relating to his fellow men. In describing two guests in her Swiss home recently, a friend of ours said of them: 'It was easy to build a personal relationship with them; their "Yes" was Yes and their "No" was No.' This couple were not Christian, but their example is an object-lesson in integrity. Paul was held firm in his own integrity by the way God has behaved so positively and reliably towards him. So far from acting 'according to the flesh', he strove to make his plans and live out his life according to the example of Jesus, who had challenged all his disciples in this uncompromising fashion: 'Simply let your "Yes" be "Yes", and your "No", "No"; anything beyond this comes from the evil one' (Matt. 5: 37 NIV).

KEEPING MY WORD

One practical example from my own experience of this straightforward integrity may well help at this point.

When we originally agreed to leave Cape Town to join
Michael Green at St Aldate's, Oxford, I promised
informally that we would come for five years. After three
years in Oxford, we felt increasingly unsettled and ready to
move. A number of possibilities emerged but, always after
a lot of uncertainty, each one faded away. If I am honest
with myself, I always had my original undertaking at the
back of my mind – but was often unwilling to take it
seriously. There were many rationalisations to justify
forgetting it, and not a few voices (Christian ones)
advocating a move.

At the end of the three-year period, one of my colleagues
at St Aldate's actually preached a sermon on the teaching
of Jesus just quoted, 'Let your Yes be Yes'. In that
distinctive way in which the Holy Spirit constantly brings
the word of God home to our hearts, I knew as I listened to
that sermon that the Lord was telling me, 'Keep your
promise and stay here for the full five years.' Thus, in
addition to my original promise, I had a clear message
through God's word. In my disobedience, I spent a lot of
time and energy considering action which would have
lacked basic integrity. I would have been acting 'like a
worldly man, ready to say Yes and No at once' (2 Cor. 1:
17). In spite of my repeated unwillingness to act like God
in Jesus, he in his patient grace kept me from actually
behaving in such an unChristian way.

We live in a generation and a culture where basic
honesty is at a premium. To keep your word and to be
reliable in very humdrum and routine responsibilities is a
rare commodity.

Bernard Levin, writing his column in *The Times*
recently, recounts a fascinating true story. An American
policeman was having lunch not long ago at a café he
regularly visited; over the time he had been going there he
had become friendly with one of the waitresses, who
always attended to him. While he was eating, he was
filling in his entry in the local public lottery, putting

down numbers as he thought of them. He turned to the waitress and asked her to call out some numbers at random. She did so, and with them he completed the coupon. As he left the café, he told the waitress that, if he won anything with his lottery ticket, he would give her half.

His entry won the first prize, which was six million dollars. The day after he got the money, he went into the café and gave the girl exactly half of it. Rebuked by the cynical for such wanton generosity, he said that a promise was a promise, and added that anyway friendship was more important than money.

Bernard Levin's postscript to the story is equally intriguing: 'That policeman kept faith with his friend the waitress. But he kept another faith: with his own soul (which is the breath which animates the voice we call conscience).'[8]

In the daily life of a local church, one is constantly falling foul of people who fail to keep their promises over very ordinary tasks. Frequently, the reason lies in a person's unwillingness to put himself to any inconvenience. He may have promised to help in cleaning the church or in delivering some letters, but then something else crops up which he really wants to do, and his promise counts for nothing. This lack of integrity, which is really nothing more or less than behaving like anyone else who is not a Christian (and many people *without* any Christian commitment show greater integrity), is arguably the single most serious obstacle to the steady growth of the Church. In the glow of lovely spiritual experiences, these unglamorous priorities seem to have gone by the board – to be replaced by an unattractive, unadmitted policy of doing what we please, not what pleases Christ.

This attitude has been spawned, I believe, by the more full-grown refusal to embrace anything which is unpleasant, painful or difficult. The mentality which says, 'I will only do it if I feel like doing it', is fundamentally alien to the spirit of Christ, as well as completely in line with the mood of this – and every – age. We may not realise how seriously the world has the Church in its stranglehold. It is this ignorance which is more frightening than the mentality itself.

3

PASTORAL CARE

During the last twenty years, there has been a most welcome concentration in many local churches on the priority of pastoral care, often linked with the more specialised ministry of counselling. There can be little doubt that there is, in general, far better support and encouragement for individual Christians as a result of this development. As in secular counselling and therapy, approaches in the Church have varied considerably both in their underlying premisses and in their actual techniques.

For example, two of the most respected and followed Christian practitioners in the USA are Gary Collins[1] and Jay Adams.[2] Adams is strongly against any non-directive approach, advocating what he terms 'nouthetic counselling' as the way of instilling biblical truth (and no other) into an individual's attitudes and behaviour. Collins, on the other hand, while equally strong on the need for biblical content in counselling, seeks to draw from the insights of many secular psychiatrists in a far less directive way than Adams.

But it is not simply in the more specialised area of counselling that we find varied emphases and practices. In the day-to-day care within a local church, we discover different kinds of personal support and ministry. Much has been written in favour and in criticism of close personal 'discipling'. In some churches a clearly-structured pattern of overseeing has been developed, whereby each individual is the specific responsibility of another Christian, the intention being that the older Christian should have had experience of spiritual life and growth over a considerable period of time. Unfortunately, the facts of such churches quash the ideals and one often finds Christians who are young in both years and experience carrying responsibility far in excess of their maturity.

In churches where there is not such a marked lack of Christian experience different difficulties can arise. One common problem emerges when there are, perhaps, several people competent and mature in pastoral care who become almost like gurus to the congregation. This may not be due to any desire on their part, let alone plan, to become the experts. It is more likely to be the inevitable result of needy people wanting/needing to find someone to provide the answers for their problems and to make the decisions for them. Individuals in need then tend to become dependent on one particular Christian in a way that is constructive for neither. Indeed, there may actually be a mutual dependency – the 'needy' person must have that individual to care for them, the 'maturer' Christian needs to be wanted.

STAND ON YOUR OWN FEET

On the other hand – and often in reaction to any 'heavy' counselling methods – it is easy to slip into a fairly laissez-faire attitude to growth in discipleship. Such an attitude basically expects Christians to stand on their own feet and the pastoral staff is known to be around in emergencies. This approach means that pastoral care is substantially interpreted as crisis-counselling, apart from the spin-off from house meetings and other gatherings.

In 2 Corinthians Paul is writing predominantly from his pastor's heart. All the way through the letter we can find important and valuable clues about pastoral care, particularly in the passage from 1: 3 to 2: 11. We will look at this in some detail in this chapter. The general truth which permeates Paul's pastoral relationship with the church at Corinth once again illustrates the overall theme of the letter – there is both suffering and glory in the way Christians relate to one another, and we shall not break through to taste the glory of fellowship renewed in the love of God by his Spirit unless we are ready to share the suffering involved in expressing that love.

Paul suffered more in his pastoral care for the Corinthian Christians than anywhere else. Yet he came closer to them as a result. It probably ought to be stressed, also, that Christian growth, especially in personal relationships, is not so much a matter of solving problems, as learning to live through them in the grace which God provides. We have allowed ourselves to be conditioned, through living in a problem-orientated and problem-solving society, into judging the health of a church fellowship by the number of personal and interpersonal problems which have been resolved. I doubt whether this is what Christian maturity is all about. I doubt even more whether unbelieving but interested outsiders would be particularly impressed if we did solve such problems. They are far more concerned to see a community of people who are clearly as fallible and frail as themselves, but who have discovered how God's love can inhabit such frail, fallible human beings. We do not need, therefore, to hide our weaknesses, but rather to let God be God in the midst of them all.

Paul provides us with some important clues. He is specifically concerned in this passage about the likely pain to the Corinthians if he visited them again. His time among them had never been painless. In addition, his correspondence had usually been conceived and absorbed in pain on both sides. Pain irradiated their relationship. There comes a time when, in any relationship, there has been enough pain and the wisest thing is to withdraw and allow space for the wounds to heal. That is not failure, but sanctified common sense – and the way of love. Paul believed he had reached such a place with the Corinthians, 'it was to spare you that I refrained from coming to Corinth' (1: 23).

LIVING IN THE LIGHT

Again, it is worth noting Paul's complete transparency before God in this decision. He explicitly invites the light of God's all-seeing truth to shine into his heart as he makes up his mind: 'I call God to witness against me' (1: 23). Pastoral care supremely requires such integrity before God.

This becomes even more plain when we note Paul's overriding concern in all his dealings with the Corinthians, as expressed succinctly in 1: 24. A helpful paraphrase would read: 'Not that we are lords with the right to overrule your faith, but we are your colleagues, working alongside you for your joy. Why? Because, if you are going to stand firm, you will stand by your faith.' This rule of life for those with pastoral care of others needs thorough examination. It will bring life to and through pastors of churches, elders, bishops, home-group leaders, Sunday School teachers, Christian parents and school-teachers – anyone, indeed, entrusted with the pastoral care of individuals.

Paul is determined not to dominate or manipulate. The word he uses for 'lording it' is the verb from the Greek noun for 'Lord' as applied uniquely and incontrovertibly to Jesus in the New Testament – I believe over 400 times. It was the Greek form of 'imperator', the Latin title for the Roman emperor. Even more significantly, it is the Greek word used in the Septuagint (the Greek translation of the Old Testament) for Yahweh, the name of God as revealed to Moses at his commissioning.[3] Paul is unambiguously telling the Corinthians: 'Jesus is Lord, your Lord, and I will do nothing to usurp his pre-eminent place in your lives.' That is a searching truth for any person entrusted with pastoral responsibility, because it is all too easy to take the place of Jesus in someone's affections or allegiance.

Paul says that he will not be the lord of their 'faith'. Jesus is the author, as well as the completer, of faith.[4] He evokes and deepens faith in those who look to him. In such faith any Christian is able to grow up to salvation, into all that God has for him as his child. It is only such faith in Jesus which brings true growth. The whole of our lives, in general and in detail, is intended to be lived by faith in the Lord Jesus. If, in our pastoral care, we influence in any way a fellow Christian to act, think or speak because we say so, we are undercutting his faith. We should, therefore, aim all the time to enable others to see Jesus, what obedience to him implies in this or that situation, and then to get out of the way so that they can exercise their own faith in him.

FELLOW-WORKERS

In rejecting any attitude, let alone position, of dominance, Paul positively describes himself as a colleague, a fellow-worker, labouring alongside the Corinthians as an equal. This self-humbling by the apostle is a salutary lesson in today's climate of up-front leadership. Paul was not alone in this determination. Peter, out of his own bitter experience, writes with equal candour: 'So I exhort the elders among you, as a fellow elder and a witness of the sufferings of Christ as well as a partaker in the glory that is to be revealed. Tend the flock of God that is your charge, not by constraint but willingly, not for shameful gain but eagerly, not as domineering over those in your charge but being examples to the flock' (1 Pet. 5: 1-3).[5]

Equally, the writer of the letter to the Hebrews, in urging a proper respect for Christian leaders who have expounded God's word consistently, exhorts his readers to 'consider the outcome of their life and imitate their *faith*' (Heb. 13: 7-8) (my italics). It is faith which the New Testament writers steadily stress and want to see deepened in every believer. Any tendency by those in leadership to dominate, or to manipulate by force of personality (often unconsciously), prevents the growth of faith.

More positively, Paul describes himself as working side by side with the Christians at Corinth 'for your joy'. The joy of the Christian is neither a superficial happiness nor a temperamental outlook. It is the gift of God deep in the inner being of his children, experienced as we abide in Christ in loving obedience, seeing our prayer answered and knowing the unshakable presence of the Lord.[6] Paul wanted to see the Christians in his care with freedom to know that joy.

When the conductor Sir Georg Solti was asked for the best advice he had been given, he recounted some words spoken to him in 1948 by Richard Strauss when the composer was a very old man: 'The conductor must not enjoy himself too much when he is conducting; he must let the public enjoy themselves.'[7]

When so much modern discipleship seems to have become a chore and an effort, those who have responsibility for others need to ask searching questions about the nature of our pastoral care. Are we taking ourselves as pastors too seriously, so seriously that the joy is missing all round?

The writer of the letter to the Hebrews describes Christian leaders as those who 'are keeping watch over your souls, as men who will have to give account', and then urges them in a surprising manner, 'Let them do this *joyfully*, and not sadly, for that would be of no advantage to you' (Heb. 13: 17) (my italics).

I was recently listening to an experienced Christian talking about the impact of a pastor on his life. One particular phrase has stuck with me: 'He gave me room to be myself and I felt relaxed in his presence.' That seems to me to be an excellent goal in pastoral care and I sensed, from the way this remark was passed, that for one Christian at least this was a rare occurrence.

To be this kind of pastor, the one who comes alongside as an equal and works to release our faith and joy in the Lord, requires at least two other qualities – the ability to feel pain and the readiness to bring discipline. Paul is explicit about both in this paragraph of his letter.

AFFLICTION AND ANGUISH

His pain is a frequent motif: the word describes a hidden sorrow which is the inevitable bedfellow of Christian joy. In pastoral care it is unavoidable, unless we operate with a clinical detachment that is more professional than personal. Even with the necessary distance involved in letter-writing, Paul testifies to 'much affliction and anguish of heart and with many tears' (2 Cor. 2: 4). James Denney's comment on this is very penetrating: 'We shall not make others weep for that for which we have not wept. That is the law which God has established in the world; he submitted to it himself in the person of his Son, and he requires us to submit to it.'[8]

It is this pain in pastoral care which is above all, I believe, the reason for what is being increasingly termed 'burn-out' in the caring professions. We are not able to go on indefinitely caring for those in whose sufferings we identify and for whose welfare we feel deeply. Such ministry takes its steady toll. Yet it cannot be avoided. Instead of trying to side-step the pain or diminish its impact by non-involvement, it seems far wiser to pace ourselves more sensibly, to avoid too heavy a workload, to learn to recognise the symptoms of burn-out, and (if at all possible) to take time out from such exhausting ministry for renewal and rest.

The second requirement for the kind of pastoral care Paul is demonstrating is the readiness to bring discipline where necessary. The particular situation mentioned cannot be precisely determined. Clearly a member of the fellowship at Corinth had transgressed the law of Christ and had been duly disciplined. Paul is now certain that his punishment has been sufficient, and that it is time to assure the person of full forgiveness: 'reaffirm your love for him' (2: 9). As Christians we are often remiss in bringing discipline and over-rigorous in our reluctance to accept a restored miscreant. Both the firmness and the forgiveness are essential to proper pastoral care in the love of God.

God's love does not balk at exercising a firm corrective when one of his children goes against his will. Like a wise human father, his love moves him to bring clear and consistent discipline. Many Christians are unsure of their acceptance with God, because those to whom they look for pastoral care are reluctant to point out areas or attitudes of disobedience. Equally, those who have been properly disciplined find it difficult to believe that God still loves them, because a cloud always seems to be hanging over them in the Christian community, long after they have fulfilled the requirements of their discipline.

NO SHORT CUTS

It can be readily seen why both the ability to feel pain and the readiness to bring discipline will come only with difficulty to those who are reluctant to see what is unpleasant as essential to Christian discipleship. We all want to reach the glory with the minimum of suffering. When it comes to pastoral care, there are no short cuts to bypass the pain of working through the suffering involved at the heart of people's lives.

Only the love of God can inspire such pastoral care. So it is no surprise that Paul stresses 'the abundant love I have for you'. He actually uses an intensive form of the word translated 'abundant', presumably because he wants the Corinthians to know that his anguish and tears come from a love for them which is even fuller than usual. It is a theme which comes consistently through Paul's letters to the various churches in which he was involved.[9] Because pastoral care can degenerate into a drudgery and a thing to be dreaded, we need constantly to pray for the Holy Spirit to renew in us God's love for his people.

One final comment needs to be made about pastoral care: the way we deal with one individual has its impact and repercussions on the fellowship as a whole. Paul draws this conclusion from the need for the believers at Corinth as a whole to welcome back unconditionally the Christian who has been under discipline. By God's express design we are linked to one another as members of Christ's body. If there is a cold remoteness where there should be warm support and sensitivity, the whole fellowship will suffer. If discipline is either avoided or unjustly extended beyond the proper time, the Christian family as a whole is damaged. That gives Satan a flying start in an area at which he is supremely interested and adept – but the activity of Satan will be tackled later.[10] If, like Paul, we are 'not ignorant of his designs' (2: 11), we shall examine carefully the quality of pastoral care in our churches.

4

TRIUMPH AND TRIUMPHALISM

Many Christians – including myself – find constant victory an elusive experience, especially the kind which some people seem to enjoy most of the time, if their claims have any substance. It goes deeper than that, because accounts of spiritual triumph and continuous blessing begin to grate hard. The stories of success and happiness are either short on credibility or long on superficiality. It is easy to become cynical, which is the surest route to personal barrenness of soul.

Some people need to boost their own low morale and self-image by recounting recurrent moments of blessing. They even reach the point at which negative experiences genuinely do not register on their primary consciousness. I can personally understand this, because I am temperamentally an optimist and instinctively an idealist – as my friends never tire, with a measure of impatience, of telling me. But my involvement in pastoral ministry over the years has unearthed innumerable Christians who honestly cannot cope with those who, as they themselves perceive it, are shallow and even dishonest in the way they recount their experience of God.

In this chapter I want to look carefully at what Paul says about Christian victory, so that we can be clearer about the confidence we can properly have as children of God. I have found that the best way to do this is by way of several word-studies: five words stand out in the passage from 2 Corinthians 2: 14 to 3: 18. These are: triumph (2: 14), confidence (3: 4), sufficiency (or competence, or adequacy, 3: 5, 6), boldness (3: 12) and freedom (3: 17). There is another, perhaps all-embracing, word which occurs on several occasions – glory or splendour (the word is the same in the Greek text). It seems likely that Paul sees this glory as expressed when Christians know and reveal triumph, confidence, sufficiency, boldness and freedom. It is vital, therefore, to understand more of what he means by all six words.

THE EXPERIENCE OF MOSES

In talking of glory and splendour, Paul deliberately harks back to Moses' experience of God.[1] 'The Lord used to speak to Moses face to face, as a man speaks to his friend' (Exod. 33: 11); but Moses wanted to know God better (33: 13), especially in the wake of the indescribable disaster involving the Golden Calf (32: 1–35), through which the people of Israel had summarily broken the covenant which he had just received from God on Mount Sinai. Moses' burning question was: 'How can I and my people again get through to God? How can God get through to us?' The two tablets of stone, on which the terms of the covenant between God and his people had been recorded, Moses had smashed in his anger at their brazen idolatry. Was there a way back into the presence and glory of God? An old, timeless and ever-contemporary question.

Yes, there was. By the sovereign action of God's grace, Moses was summoned again to the top of the mountain, the covenant was renewed, and Moses returned to the people, not knowing that 'the skin of his face shone because he had been talking with God' (34: 29). The people were so awed by Moses' appearance that they drew near to hear what he had to say, only after he had expressly ordered them to do so.

Once God's instructions had been passed on to the people, Moses put a veil over his face and he only removed it whenever he entered 'the tent of meeting' to speak with God. His regular visits to the tent of meeting were necessary to keep the splendour of God's glory shining on his face. Paul makes the wry comment that Moses kept the veil on while he was in the camp, 'so that the Israelites might not see the end of the fading splendour' (2 Cor. 3: 13).

Now there are several important points to make about Moses' experience of God, according to Paul. It was for a limited time. It was limited to Moses alone. It was limited to a certain geographical place. As a result of these three fundamental limitations, the people were not merely excluded from God's glorious presence; they had their sinfulness and condemnation before God heavily underlined by this exclusion. One further limitation in Moses' experience of God's glory is crucial to appreciate – that the glory shone only in his face, not out of his inner being.

This sequence of limitations, asserts Paul, had its inexorable sequel in his own day – and, we might add, in our own day: 'whenever Moses is read [i.e. the Law and the old covenant] a veil lies over their minds' (2 Cor. 3: 15–16). In other words, the veil over Moses' face has had its counterpart over the minds of those locked in to the old covenant: his encounter with God effectively confirmed the people's non-encounter with God, which was due to their hardness of heart (2 Cor. 3: 14). This non-encounter is repeated, says Paul, in the experience of all those who refuse to believe: 'In their case the god of this world has blinded the minds of unbelievers, to keep them from seeing the light of the gospel of the glory of Christ, who is the likeness of God' (2 Cor. 4: 4).

LIVING IN PRISON

This was the prison in which Paul himself (in his adherence to the written code of Judaism) had been confined for so long – exclusion from the glorious presence of God, condemnation by a holy God for his unrighteousness, with only fleeting glimpses through his prison-bars of the glory which might be. But now 'God has shone in our hearts, to give the light of the knowledge of the glory of God in the face of Christ' (2 Cor. 4: 6). Like Moses, Paul wanted to know God better. In Jesus Christ God answered Paul's longing in a way that was permanent, not fleeting; personal and internal, not superficial; liberating and fulfilling, not limiting and confining.

The glory of God shone in the face of Jesus Christ because it was internal in his character. Through the Spirit we all have access to an inner transformation which Moses never knew. Jesus makes it possible for everyone to know God's glory in their inmost being – not just the odd spiritual giant like Paul or Peter. God has broken through our sin and stubbornness in his Son, Jesus.

That is the new covenant in the Spirit (3: 6); that is the glorious gospel, of which Paul knows he has been made a minister (4: 4–6). This is the splendour and the glory to which Paul addresses himself and his readers in this remarkable passage. It is the ministry – indeed, the joy and delight – of the Holy Spirit to make this glory real in the hearts and lives of believers. That is why the ministry of the Spirit is so fundamental and so glorious, because it is he who both enables us to *see* the glory of God, and gradually transforms us into becoming like Jesus (3: 18), and thus to *share* the glory of God.

In case it is objected that this emphasis on seeing the glory of God is escapist and narrowly pietistic, we should note Paul's stress on the ministry of the Spirit in the new covenant as being 'the dispensation of righteousness' (3:

9). Righteousness in the Bible essentially means a right relationship with God motivating right dealings with one another. To allow the Spirit to minister righteousness to us is, therefore, no 'glory-trip', opting out of the harshness of the world's sin and suffering; on the contrary, it is opting in to the righteousness which he requires and alone can produce. It means drawing on the resources of the Holy Spirit to get our relationships sorted out, to come alongside the deprived and the oppressed, to be ruthless in dealing with everything within ourselves which impedes such change.

I am aware that this discussion of glory is difficult to follow and could easily be seen as remote and unreal. For two reasons I believe it is essential to stay with it and to take it further. The first is very mundane. Many Christians use the word 'glorious' today in very vapid ways. It has become a cliche to describe the indescribable – a glorious time of worship, a glorious experience of real fellowship, a glorious day/view/moment. We have devalued the coinage.

The second reason for pursuing the theme of glory lies in my own conviction that deeper understanding will open the door to deeper experience of God. It will not guarantee such an experience: whatever is asserted by some Christians, understanding guarantees nothing. Just as suffering is essential to Christian vocation, so is glory. I hope the next five word-studies will shed more light.

1. Triumph. 'But thanks be to God who in Christ always leads us in triumph' (2 Cor. 2: 14). This expression of praise has been constantly echoed on the lips of Christians, in genuine thanksgiving to God for his guidance and victory. As Denney comments, 'He who has not thanked God with a whole heart does not know what joy is.'[2]

And yet we may be missing out on what Paul really means, if we interpret his explosion of gratitude as a personal testimony to outward success in his ministry.

The English translation of this verse normally gives the impression of Christians being victorious conquerors through Jesus, sharing in his triumph. It is then used to spark off accounts of wonderful results in Christian service, of large numbers converted or healed, or of tangible success in what we have undertaken. Emphasis is placed in such descriptions on outward and worldly evidence. This is the attitude which is properly called 'triumphalism'. What Paul understands by using the word 'triumph' is significantly different.

It is not disputed that Paul has in his mind an event which was common enough in the Roman Empire, the triumphal procession of a Roman general on returning home after a foreign campaign. Usually in the capital itself, but sometimes in provincial cities like Ephesus or Philippi, these occasions were very impressive and memorable. The general paraded all the booty of war – gold and silver, food and drink, treasures and status, prisoners of war, survivors, women and children. At the tail-end of the procession came the prize exhibit – the vanquished general himself. The whole ceremony was intended to glorify the conqueror, as each successive trophy demonstrated his triumph.

FORCED TO CAPITULATE

Many Christians see themselves as seated alongside the conquering Jesus, with all his enemies in disgrace beneath them. This is not Paul's imagery. On the contrary, he sees himself as one of the defeated enemies, as a captive in Christ's triumphal march. Christ is leading him, Paul, in triumph – but the triumph is Christ's, or God's in Christ. Paul thanks God because Jesus has forced him to capitulate. Paul is, therefore, assuming the position and attitude of a slave, a slave in chains – because to the Romans all captured prisoners automatically became slaves (unless the emperor in his gracious favour rescinded the law for a specific individual). Paul rejoices to be called a slave of Jesus, not to be a mighty conqueror. In fact, Paul sees himself, in a parallel passage (1 Cor. 4: 9), to be like the captured general, who was doomed to death, not slavery.

Of course, to become a slave of Jesus is to know freedom and victory, as George Matheson in his blindness wrote so evocatively:

> Make me a captive, Lord,
> and then I shall be free;
> force me to render up my sword,
> and I shall conqueror be.[3]

But I wonder if I am alone in detecting an unhealthy and a wrong spirit of pride in a certain kind of spirituality prevalent today.

Other perspectives from Paul's use of the triumph imagery endorse the emphasis on humility, submission and obedience, rather than on reigning in victory and majesty. In his first letter to the Corinthians, when combating their tendency to think they had already arrived into full possession of their inheritance in Christ, Paul employs the same simile of a Roman triumph. He reflects, with a touch of ruefulness and a sharp dash of irony, 'Already you are filled! Already you have become rich! Without us you have become kings! And would that you did reign, so that we might share the rule with you!' (1 Cor. 4: 8). Paul is clearly debunking the triumphalist tendencies of the Corinthian Christians. He wants them to play down, if not surrender, any notion of being triumphant kings and rulers. Roman emperors often awarded themselves, either directly or through influencing the senate, special titles after a successful campaign. We may be in danger of the same pride.

THE AROMA OF CHRIST

Even more salutary is the context of Paul's shout of thanksgiving in 2 Corinthians 2: 14. In the phrases which follow and fill out his expression of gratitude, we can see nothing but a sense of unworthiness and of awed privilege to be a captive of Christ. At Roman triumphant processions, a good deal of incense was burned to accompany the parade. The scent of the incense reached the spectators long before the procession actually arrived. Paul uses the image of this aroma to make an extraordinarily powerful statement: 'through us (i.e. his captives) [God] spreads the fragrance of the knowledge of him [Jesus] everywhere'. This is the whole purpose in God's capturing us by his love through Christ.

Denney comments: 'Nothing is so unsuppressible, nothing so pervasive, as a fragrance. Not till God leads us unresistingly in triumph will the sweet savour go forth.'[4] The keyword here is surely 'unresistingly'. Until we rejoice to be the prisoners of Jesus, we kick and fight against his authority. Consequently, there is no attractive aroma about our discipleship. As we unresistingly allow Jesus to be Lord (the word means 'emperor'), God can spread knowledge of himself far and wide through Jesus now freely at work within us.

This aroma has opposite effects on different people. To those who are perishing because of their refusal to bow the knee to Jesus as Lord, the fragrance which joyfully obedient Christians spread is the stench of death – their own spiritual separation from God, just as the veil on Moses' face underlined to the people that they were cut off from God by their rebelliousness.

To those, on the other hand, who have opened up their lives to Jesus and want to know him more thoroughly as Lord, the same fragrance spells life and peace. It confirms the truth as it is in Jesus. In other words, the spiritual condition of those within reach determines whether the aroma is repulsive or attractive, whether it reminds them of the grave or of God's glory.

I had an experience with my wife which illustrates this. When I first began to take her out with serious intent, she often wore a perfume called (aptly) 'Ma Griffe' or 'My Talons'. That perfume, as perfumes do, often wafted itself in my direction as a beautiful reminder of being alive and in love. On the first day of our honeymoon, I was feeling like death warmed up because I had for several days been seriously under the weather with flu. Rosemary was wearing the same perfume – and it was absolutely nauseating, achieving the result of making me feel even worse.

So Paul declares: 'We are the aroma of Christ to God among those who are being saved and among those who are perishing, to one a fragrance from death to death, to the other a fragrance from life to life' (2 Cor. 2: 15-16). No wonder he adds: 'Who is sufficient for these things?' So far from adopting a triumphalist attitude, Paul has been humbled, both by the love of Jesus (as conqueror) for a rebellious enemy, and by the sheer solemnity of his vocation as a minister of the gospel. How can any mere mortal cope with the frightening reality of putting people in touch with eternity in such uncompromising terms?

THE LOST ARE LIKE THIS

Gerard Manley Hopkins, the nineteenth-century poet, experienced 'the dark night of the soul' with peculiar intensity. His experience of such suffering may have strongly influenced his perspective of the glory of God, but out of his intense loathing of himself came an awesome insight into the eternal destiny of those who reject Christ. This is apparent in the following stanza:

I am gall, I am heartburn. God's most deep decree

Bitter would have me taste: my taste was me;
Bones built in me, flesh filled, blood brimmed the curse.
Selfyeast of spirit a dull dough sours. I see
The lost are like this, and their scourge to be
As I am mine, their sweating selves; but worse.[5]

And yet we often preach the gospel and record our successes as though nothing more is at stake than enlarging our congregation and increasing the budget – 'and praise the Lord for his blessing!' What about those who do not respond, who are perishing and on the way to eternal death, confirmed in their rebelliousness? Will that fact not affect both our attitude and, as Paul stresses, our handling of God's word? (2 Cor. 2: 17).[6]

Paul wants us to understand that he is profoundly grateful to the Lord for keeping him, in spite of his own fickleness and pride, in captivity to Christ. In verses 12 and 13 of this same chapter, he admits that he failed to take a God-given opportunity to preach the gospel at Troas, because he was so snarled up in his own personal problems. He failed the Lord at Troas: 'But thanks be to God who in Christ at all times leads us in triumph' (2 Cor. 2: 14). God did not leave him to his own rebellious, selfish devices; he steadily drew him onwards as his captive, kicking as he went. That is the glory of God, shown to us and shared with us in Jesus.

2. *Confidence.* 'Such is the confidence we have through Christ toward God' (2 Cor. 3: 4). Any confidence which is not through Christ is self-confidence. Any confidence which *is* through Christ will necessarily be towards God. The only way to find confidence towards God is through Christ. At least these three truths are implicit in Paul's simple statement.

Here, as in the whole of this passage, Paul is thinking of his own experience of God by contrast with that of Moses. Moses did not have any such confidence towards God. As we read on in the Exodus narrative, we discover that Moses

was given by God very precise commands about construc-
ting the tabernacle and the tent of meeting. After doing
everything which God had told him, he still could not
enter the tent of meeting.

The narrative runs like this: 'Then the cloud covered the
tent of meeting, and the glory of the Lord filled the
tabernacle. And Moses was not able to enter the tent of
meeting, because the cloud abode upon it, and the glory of
the Lord filled the tabernacle' (Exod. 40: 34-5). The Lord
led them all onwards towards the Promised Land, but
Moses knew no confidence towards God and the people
knew none either. Moses actually was denied the privilege
of leading them into the Promised Land.

Paul rejoiced that the glory of God had shone, not only
in his own heart, but also in the lives of the Christians at
Corinth. They had been transformed by the Spirit of the
living God, and they themselves were living proof of
God's glory at work in ordinary people to transform them
into a vivid and descriptive 'letter from Christ' (2 Cor. 3: 2,
3), so that anyone could read the message of the gospel in
their very lives.

TRANSFORMED LIVES

What gave Paul complete confidence in God was this
manifest transformation in the lives of those who
responded to the gospel. When we do not have such
incontrovertible evidence of the Spirit around us, it is very
easy to develop a confidence which is not really through
Christ towards God. It is, on the contrary, a rather brash
self-advertisement which must let people know what God
has been doing through me. We may use language which
sounds acceptable, but the net result becomes a catalogue
of the way God is using us. The impression then given is
that we are important, perhaps even indispensable, to God
for the work of his kingdom.

In spite of all his agony about the church at Corinth, Paul was confident enough in God to leave the results to him. This did not come easily to the apostle, and at the beginning of chapter 3 (2 Corinthians) he acknowledges that he might be on the verge of once more commending himself, rather than commending Christ. To Paul, an essential part of the glory of God in the gospel was the freedom it gave him to leave his reputation and eternal destiny securely in God's hands. Whenever he found himself veering towards self-advertisement, self-justification or even self-defence, he realised he was moving off the solid ground of what God had done in Christ.

We should do well to ask ourselves whether we need outward success or public recognition to establish our basic confidence. Are we firmly grounded on what God has done in Christ and is working into the warp and woof of people's lives by his Spirit?

I occasionally find myself, after a particularly stressful day in the parish, taking a hard look at my life – where it has come from and where it is going. I usually get round to wondering whether I shall actually make it, not simply to the end, but into heaven. I think of all the opportunities missed or ignored, all the laziness, pride and prayerlessness. My confidence ebbs. In such introspective moments the temptation is strong to start comparing myself with other Christians – with Bill Bloggs, Joe Soap and Mary Poppins. I know they have the same problems and failures as I do, but I know God could not ultimately write them all off – and I am not any worse than they are, so I convince myself. I end up fairly confident that everything will be all right in the end, because I have been comparing myself (favourably) with others. It is, of course, very easy to end up, on the contrary, in destructive self-condemnation after comparing oneself with others. In either situation I am standing on sinking sand.

This simple story might help to illustrate how we can be subtly moved away from confidence through Christ towards God. There is not a trace of genuinely Christian confidence in the experience I have just related – yet it is a not uncommon mental trip among the many cul-de-sacs we allow ourselves to enter, instead of leaning exclusively on Christ's death, resurrection and the gift of his Spirit.

3. *Sufficiency*. In facing the implications of being a minister of the gospel, Paul has already declared: 'Who is sufficient for these things?' (2 Cor. 2: 16). He has been profoundly moved by his own inadequacy to do anything of significance for the kingdom of God. We cannot know whether Paul lived continuously in this awareness of inadequacy, but it certainly holds the key to ministry in the power of the Spirit.

Perhaps the most revealing aspect of Paul's consciousness of his inadequacy is the fact that he stresses it at this comparatively late stage in his ministry. He did not lack experience. He had been exposed to most possibilities. He had been into and come out of a long list of challenges, perils and no-go situations. He had been at the end of his tether on several occasions. Still he felt and knew himself to be completely inadequate for Christian ministry. Experience never makes us adequate or competent. In fact, it is more likely that our experience will subtly make us truly inadequate, because we develop a familiarity which breeds self-sufficiency: and that is the death-knell of ministry in the power of the Holy Spirit.

FAMILIAR TERRITORY

The contrast with Moses is once more very suggestive. Over the long-drawn-out years of leading the people of Israel through the wilderness, Moses developed an understandably resigned attitude to the trials and tribulations of bringing his people into the Promised Land. After forty years he had seen most things and heard it all. When the people began to grumble yet again about the lack of water, Moses did not listen carefully enough when he brought the complaint to God. At the beginning of the forty years, when they had asked for water, God had told him to *strike* a rock with his rod and water would gush out. This time, God told him to take his rod and *tell* the rock to yield water.

Presumably because he was listening more closely to his own experience than to the explicit instructions of the Lord, Moses repeated his previous methods and struck the rock again – and twice for good measure. But God had not told him to do that and the consequences for Moses were devastating: 'Therefore you shall not bring this assembly into the land which I have given them.'[7]

God creates competent ministers of his new covenant. By definition – i.e., because the new covenant is 'in the Spirit' (2 Cor. 3: 6), who can never be programmed, predicted or presumed upon – we need habitually to renounce any tendency to think that we have what it takes, and to go on asking for the Spirit's power for each and every situation.

ROTE AND REPETITION

The alternative is as frightening as it is frequently indiscernible: when we carry out our ministry by rote, repeating what we have done before in similar situations, we dispense not life in the Spirit, but death. Those on the receiving end sense, if they cannot explain, an oppressiveness in what we do and say, 'the written code kills' (2 Cor. 3: 6). Nobody involved in Christian ministry can be unfamiliar with this fact. Who has not repeated a sermon because it was well received last time? Who has not offered to a person in need advice which proved beneficial to another in similar need? Who has not made a decision, not after prayer and in sensitivity to the Spirit, but according to action taken successfully in a parallel situation some time previously?

Like Moses, the real problem lies in the impressive and

convincing results which such actions can achieve, not so much in any necessary ineffectiveness. The salutary fact is that ministry which is not led and inspired by the Spirit can, in one sense, produce the goods. What is needed is the odd person close to us, who will let us know unequivocally when we are dealing out death, not life. At the same time we must examine ourselves for any trace of self-confidence or mechanical approach in our ministry. Only the fresh renewal of the Holy Spirit can guarantee sufficiency, and thus keep us in touch with the glory of God.

When Paul declares, 'Our competence [sufficiency] is from God' (2 Cor. 3: 5), it is quite possible that his thorough education in the Old Testament lies behind his affirmation. One of the most striking titles of God is El Shaddai, which literally means 'the God who suffices'. This title could well have been ingrained in Saul the Pharisee's heart. Three Old Testament personalities knew God as the God who suffices, the God who is enough. Abraham, for example, is reassured about God's reliability when he is on the brink of throwing in the towel (Gen. 17: 1). Naomi, tragically bereaved of her husband and two sons, talks of the God who suffices even in her bitterness and calamity (Ruth 1: 20-1). Job aggressively questions the point of prayer to the God who suffices, recognises the need for him to keep pure before this God, and ultimately receives a confrontive rebuke from the God who is enough (Job 21: 15; 31: 2; 40: 2).

If these parallels are relevant to Paul's declaration of dependence on the Lord, he is saying, 'Our sufficiency is in the One who suffices' – an obvious truth, but sadly we do not always live in the obviousness of it.

4. *Boldness.* 'Since we have such a hope, we are very bold, not like Moses . . .' (2 Cor. 3: 12-13). The Greek word used here – and on several important occasions in both Acts and Paul's letters – was used of the full citizen-rights of a Greek in his city-state. The Greeks pioneered democracy as early

as the fifth century before Christ. Their pride was in the boldness with which any citizen could say what he liked without fear of ostracism or punishment.

Because we are citizens of the kingdom of God, we belong; because we belong, we are bold to speak to God and to one another with openness and trust. This is an integral ingredient of life in the family of God, and is a fruit of his glorious love and truth having shone in our hearts in the face of Jesus Christ. Moses did not enjoy such boldness, either in conversation with God or in contact with his contemporaries. He was not free to relate in this way; he had (literally) to cover up.

Christians, on the other hand, have unimpeded access to 'the throne of grace' (Heb. 4: 16). We can come to God at any time, not hesitatingly or with heads hanging, but boldly through the work of Jesus on the Cross. There, before this throne of grace and glory, we are free to pour out our hearts before him – a boldness which should characterise Christian worship. When God's people exercise their privileges in Jesus in this way, the glory of the Lord permeates their worship.

Equally, the glory of God can be readily seen in a fellowship of believers in whom this boldness with one another is becoming a reality. Speaking the truth in love – as Paul describes it elsewhere (Eph. 4: 15) – is not necessarily a mark of those fellowships who talk most openly about the work of the Spirit. Often this is due to a tendency to tell only success stories which, once allowed unimpeded room to grow, makes bold truth-speaking in a loving spirit extremely difficult to maintain.

OPEN CRITICISM

Essential to such boldness, whether in the political sphere or in the family of God, is the ability to question and to criticise. Yet it is precisely these activities which usually produce accusations of disloyalty and 'a critical spirit'. It is surely important in a local church that such bold speaking is encouraged. If a message or an action has the genuine mark of the Spirit upon it, it can stand up to such questioning. If it does not have that mark, the sooner it is revealed to be purely human the better. Otherwise, a conspiracy of blind acceptance and bland approval soon clouds over the glory of God.

5. *Freedom.* '... and where the Spirit of the Lord is, there is freedom' (2 Cor. 3: 17). Whatever else this freedom does or does not entail, the context here makes plain that Paul is thinking mainly of the freedom to be changed into the likeness of Jesus. Whatever happened to Moses when his face shone through his encounters with the Lord, he did not know this inner freedom. The freedom at issue here, therefore, is not any imaginary freedom to do what I like, but room for God to move in my inner being to change me.

The free man is the person who observes the priority of 'beholding the glory of the Lord' (2 Cor. 3: 18) in the face of Jesus Christ. As he beholds that glory, he begins increasingly to reflect it in a character which is being gradually transformed to become like Jesus. It happens only by degrees, not all at once. It is, therefore, no part of authentic victory in Christ to talk as if any single experience puts us in the clear of all the rough-and-tumble of Christian discipleship.

RESIGNED TO BONDAGE

It is sad to hear of Christians who have become resigned to some inner bondage because they have stopped believing that God can actually change them by his Spirit. Part of the glory of God in the gospel lies in his power to transform the most intractable elements of human nature. We cannot afford to sign away such an essential aspect of God's dealings with us.

Frequently, the reason for such disillusionment lies deeper – in an unwillingness to be changed, because the cost is too great in terms of our own comforts and chosen life style. There was profound insight in Jesus's own question to the paralytic at the pool of Bethesda, 'Do you want to be healed?' (John 5: 6). We often feel we are lumbered with who we are, but we prefer it that way.

However much Paul stresses the need for us to spend time 'beholding the glory of the Lord', we must avoid the danger of thinking that by our concentration on God's glory we do the transforming. Denney steers clear of this danger when he helpfully comments: 'The transformation is not accomplished *by* beholding, but while we behold.'[8]

As we behold, so we reflect the glory of God: but it is the work of the Spirit. This fact again reinforces the paramount importance of worship. If we are not involved in worship which concentrates our attention on the glory of God in the face of Jesus Christ, we are not actually doing much at all in Christian discipleship and ministry. Why? Because such worship allows the Spirit to go on changing us, and this inner transformation is the essence of Christian growth and the basis of integrity in Christian ministry.

Triumph... confidence... sufficiency... boldness:... freedom. Each word opens up a window on what it means to express the glory of God as by his Spirit he burns it into our inner being. To this we have been called.

5

HANDLING GOD'S WORD

Now that we have taken a lengthy look both at Paul's experience of suffering and at his description of glory, it is timely to pause to consider his overall attitude to God's word. Twice in the first few chapters he has, with some feeling, disassociated himself from those who mishandle the word of God. It is clearly a subject very close to the apostle's heart.

The two passages are full of passion. They run like this – 'For we are not, like so many, pedlars of God's word; but as men of sincerity, as commissioned by God, in the sight of God we speak in Christ' (2 Cor. 2: 17).

We have renounced disgraceful, underhanded ways; we refuse to practise cunning or to tamper with God's word, but by the open statement of truth we would commend ourselves to every man's conscience in the sight of God ... For what we preach is, not ourselves, but Jesus Christ as Lord, with ourselves as your servants for Jesus' sake (2 Cor. 4: 2, 5).

Now it is easy and fashionable to accuse others of mishandling the word of God, but to carry a clean sheet oneself. None of us, of course, is guiltless and it will be useful, therefore, to notice Paul's own self-discipline in handling God's word, especially the dangers he avoids and castigates. It will become plain very soon that he points the searchlight on the *motives* of all those who are called to proclaim God's word.

WATERING DOWN THE WINE

His first expose is of those whom he calls 'pedlars' (2 Cor. 3: 17). It is a particularly vivid word, originally referring to those who watered down wine for sale in the market. Deception was involved, but also the desire to make a fat, quick profit through the deception. These dealers passed off an inferior product as the real thing, and made money out of it. Paul reckoned that many, in Corinth and elsewhere, were doing the same with the word of God. These people were taking out some of the strength and pungency of the message, adding instead insipid man-made ideas. Paul was clear that the reason was to make money: there was profit to be made in titillating men's searching minds and tantalising men's hungry souls.

The word of God is watered down today. Unpalatable aspects of the gospel, and of the whole counsel of God in the Scriptures, are played down, if not removed. The inevitability and the blessings of suffering provide one immediate example. Another frequent practice is to ignore the cost of discipleship in presenting Jesus as the big problem-solver and giver of blessings – almost a 'sugar-daddy' in the sky. Repentance has often been seriously underemphasised, or emasculated.[1] The raw challenge of Jesus to the wealthy, and his warnings about the eternal peril of letting possessions take control of us, are equally noticeable by their absence from many people's preaching.

One or two other topics are carefully avoided in certain circles, if you want to remain acceptable and approved, let alone rewarded. For example, it is easy – in certain parts of the country – to hold back on what God's word says about the demands of Jesus as Lord over and above the appeals to patriotism which have been stridently blared out recently in both Britain and America. Other so-called political issues in the plain teaching of God's word are often strenuously avoided, because it would not be worth a popular minister's position to press them.

Conversely, it was poignant to see a television programme at the beginning of 1984 which highlighted one Protestant pastor's naked courage in Northern Ireland. Against the will of his elders, in particular, this man had held out the right hand of fellowship to Catholic neighbours in the same town – and had exhorted his people from the pulpit to do the same. The cost of this obedience to God's word was seen in the constant threats to the lives of the pastor and his family.

MINISTERS OF RECONCILIATION

To preach God's word is to be a minister of reconciliation.[2] I know myself how so much in me wanted not to walk that hard road in South Africa. With security police on the fringe of any politically-suspect event, with informers in the congregation listening to and reporting any provocative material in the preaching, with the dice loaded in any case in favour of simply endorsing the status quo – it was very difficult, in a multiracial church, not to take the easy way by simply steering clear of the explosive parts of biblical truth. In any situation of conflict in any country the temptation to be a pedlar, not a preacher, of God's word is exceedingly strong.

I believe that there has been a steady watering-down of God's word in another, very different, area. I refer to the controversial aspects of the work of God's Spirit in the Church and in individual believers. In many churches certain aspects of biblical truth are simply not expounded in this regard, because they are controversial, have caused problems in the past, and are deemed too difficult to handle.

This attitude has caused a lot of splintering-off in the body of Christ, as those who want to see such themes dealt with and lived out in their local church have been compelled to go elsewhere – or simply ignore part of God's word which they feel to be as important as any other. It is a plain fact that, if a clergyman is known to have convictions on either side of the so-called 'charismatic' divide, he will not be considered for certain appointments. So some have chosen not to proclaim certain parts of God's word in order to avoid controversy.

A POLICY OF APPEASEMENT

The practice of avoiding controversy and seeking compromise is a peculiarly British trend. It has no basis in God's word. Any local church which seeks not only to handle God's word with integrity but to fashion its life according to God's word ought to be able to hold together in love and trust those who have differing opinions about the work of the Spirit. There will be controversy; there will be conflict; but that is no reason for either separation or compromise.

We cannot leave the problem of pedlars without mentioning those who appear to water down God's word for intellectual respectability, rather than for personal comfort and financial gain. For those exposed to and successful in academic disciplines, the cost of going out on a limb intellectually can hardly be overemphasised. Whether in philosophy or the natural sciences or theology (to name three subjects where the pressure seems particularly strong), contemporary academic convictions have an immensely powerful impact on Christians involved in these disciplines. It is extremely hard to step out of line, because one then risks ostracism.

In another field, that of literature, C. S. Lewis faced such pressure, although he was understandably a robust enough believer not to be unduly worried by contemporaries whose influential convictions were very different from, if not antagonistic to, his own. With the strength of kindred spirits like J. R. R. Tolkien and Charles Williams, among others of 'the Inklings', meeting weekly in a pub in Oxford, Lewis stood four-square for Christian truth in circles which were becoming increasingly and decidedly non-Christian.

Lewis was not drawn into personal animosities towards those of opposite – and widely acceptable – viewpoints, of whom the leading proponent was F. R. Leavis, from 1956 chairman of the English Faculty Board at Cambridge, on which Lewis also served. Nevertheless, when Tolkien's *Lord of the Rings* appeared about the same time, Lewis wrote to a friend affirming it to be 'the book we have all been waiting for', adding that 'it shows too, which cheers, that there are thousands left in Israel who have not bowed the knee to Leavis.'[3]

BOWING THE KNEE

It is bowing the knee to contemporary academic opinion which is the chief danger facing Christians who move in such circles. For example, will the natural scientist hold on to both the category and the reality of miracles? Will the philosopher consistently refuse to see human reason as supreme and persist in presenting Jesus as the truth? Will the academic theologian reject the tendency to divorce textual criticism from personal faith, the lecture-room from the local church, and the ivory tower from the grass-roots?

However simplistic such an analysis inevitably might appear, the kernel of the matter can be seen to lie in each

Christian's – including the Christian academic's – attitude
to the Scriptures. If these writings are regarded as
equivalent to any other literature, then whatever truth
they contain will be subject to the personal tastes or
convictions of the person reading and communicating
their message. The key question posed to us by the very
existence of the Bible is absolutely essential to grasp: Is
there such a thing as revelation from God? Has God
revealed the truth in Jesus and, derivatively, in the Bible?

If the Bible does indeed contain God's revelation of
himself, then we are in no position today to stand *above*
God's word, picking and choosing what we wish to
believe. We sit humbly *underneath* it and allow its truth to
fashion our thinking and our behaviour. This is exactly
what the theologians, among others, frequently fail to do.

For example, in the controversy surrounding the choice
of David Jenkins to be bishop of Durham in 1984, he
maintained that, in his opinion (an important and
revealing phrase), there is unlikely to have been any
historical events (such as a virgin birth or an empty tomb)
behind the apostolic Church's belief in the incarnation
and resurrection of Jesus. David Jenkins is entitled, as a
human being, to express his opinion; but his opinion
makes it plain that, as a professing Christian, he has
chosen to stand above the Scriptures and to reject certain
evidence within those writings as unreliable – to put it
mildly.

Luke and Matthew make it plain in their narrative that
Mary conceived as a virgin. All the New Testament
writers, but especially Paul in 1 Corinthians 15, patently
write in the conviction that the tomb of Jesus was empty
on Easter morning. Their world-view could not possibly
have allowed them to think of the resurrection in any other
than the orthodox and traditional manner – whatever we
may or may not believe about the principle of revelation,
i.e. God actually making himself and his ways known to
these original witnesses.

When a modern theologian dismisses the New Testament record of the birth and the resurrection of Jesus as incongruous with his personal understanding of the nature of God, he is calling the apostles both simpletons and liars. He feels free to do this, because he chooses not to accept the Bible as revealed truth from God, but as the opinions of ordinary men who were trying to interpret a life-shaking experience, but got it wrong. Revelation, for such theologians, is a non-starter in the enlightened academic world of the latter part of the twentieth century.

An indication of the seriousness of watering down and peddling God's word in this way can be seen in a very ordinary and forgettable occasion in London recently. There is an informal club of theologians and bishops, meeting occasionally to discuss matters of common interest, called 'Caps and Mitres'. The subject of one recent meeting was, 'Towards the possibility of revelation'. I personally find it deeply disturbing that Christians, called to leadership in the Church of God, cannot appreciate the appalling affront to almighty God in ever conceiving such a theme, let alone setting aside time to discuss it. Who is bowing the knee to which idol?

MIGHTY AFFIRMATIONS

There seems to be a widespread inclination to peddle and dilute God's word in this way, rather than to proclaim it. More time is spent discussing and declaring what we *cannot* be sure about than what we *can* be sure about. As American theologian, Harvey Cox, writes:

> Let us not project our own spiritual limitations onto the modern world, for it is not the world which prevents us from being religious ... Assertions ... that our modern age is uniquely incapable of faith are not lies or self-deceptions, but cries *de profundis* from those who utter

them... They are a prayer, reaching out to God...
Their *cri de coeur* tells us something important. It must
be understood... as the groan issuing from the
wounded victim who does not know why he hurts.[4]

James Denney put his own convictions with characteristic clarity: 'Nobody has any right to preach who has not
mighty affirmations to make concerning God's Son Jesus
Christ – affirmations in which there is no ambiguity.'[5] I,
for one, would be delighted to find theologians and
bishops irretrievably committed to such mighty affirmations, and preferably doing so while standing alongside
their people on the local patch, not among themselves in a
London club.

Paul's own approach to this ministry of proclaiming
God's word is unequivocal: 'as men of sincerity, as
commissioned by God, in the sight of God we speak in
Christ' (2 Cor. 2: 17). He realises the immense privilege of
being entrusted with such a ministry: it is entirely 'by the
mercy of God' (4: 1). Paul never seems to have lost this
sense of awed humility that one who had been such a fierce
opponent of the gospel should have been chosen to
proclaim it. Only such a profound sense of personal
vocation, renewed in him continuously, could have kept
him so consistently dedicated to preaching the word of
God, especially when we take into account the opposition
he encountered all the way.

For the apostle there was no possibility of entertaining
any underhand or deceitful approach to God's word. It
had been revealed to him by the Spirit and had to be passed
on unadulterated. Because it was revelation of truth from
God, not a concoction of human ideas, it was addressed to
'every man's conscience' (4: 2), not simply to men's minds.
Ideas can be freely discussed; truth challenges our whole
life style and attitudes.

JESUS CHRIST THE LORD

Paul refused to push himself forward: 'What we preach is not ourselves but Jesus Christ as Lord, with ourselves as your servants for Jesus' sake' (2 Cor. 4: 5). If we follow Paul's example, we shall be declaring not what we think or believe, but what God has done in Jesus. Ourselves we shall make available to others to be their servants.

These fundamental attitudes lay bare our inner motives in handling God's word. In another passage, Paul pinpoints several wrong motives, any one of which is likely to sound a chord in our own consciences.

For our appeal does not spring from error or uncleanness, nor is it made with guile; but just as we have been approved by God to be entrusted with the gospel, so we speak, not to please men, but to please God who tests our hearts. For we never used either words of flattery ... or a cloak for greed, as God is witness; nor did we seek glory from men ... But we were gentle among you, like a nurse taking care of her children. So, being affectionately desirous of you, we were ready to share with you not only the gospel of God but also our own selves, because you had become very dear to us (1 Thess. 2: 3–8).

The destructive and constructive motives mentioned in this passage warrant close scrutiny. Error, uncleanness, guile, pleasing men, flattery, greed, seeking men's praise: any or all of these can seep into our soul and affect the way we handle God's word. Paul's answer to such temptations was resolutely to reject such pressures, and to share himself (not simply the message) unstintingly with the people. This costly involvement between preacher and congregation is the best possible milieu for a proper handling of God's word. Each acts as a catalyst and a check for the other, and the word of God becomes the heart-beat of the Christian community. Any study of the word of God which does not spring out of this kind of Christian community life runs the severe risk of going astray.

It is not surprising, therefore, that Paul's conclusion about this relationship between preacher and congregation is so positive: 'And we also thank God constantly for this, that when you received the word of God which you heard from us, you accepted it not as the word of men, but as what it really is, the word of God, which is at work in you believers' (1 Thess. 2: 13). Every preacher since has been entrusted with this deposit of truth, as contained in the Bible, and has been commissioned to handle God's word 'in the sight of God'.

6

FACING DEATH

The tension between our call to suffering and our call to glory is nowhere more painful than in facing death. In human affairs life precedes death; in God's kingdom death precedes life. In our natural shrinking from death in its every aspect, we often miss out on the fullness of life in the kingdom of God because we are unwilling to negotiate death first.

Death is at the heart of a lengthy passage in 2 Corinthians 4: 7 to 5: 10. Paul shows that he, for one, has come to terms with death, not only as a physical inevitability but as a daily experience. He is ready to live because he is ready to die. But it is quite clear that this does not mean an easy life. In fact, the most striking aspect of his personal experience, as described in these verses, is that the sheer tension of being alive in Christ is accentuated by the glory of what he already knows and, even more, by the hope of glory in the perfection of heaven. Indeed, if it had not been for the reality of his Christian faith, Paul would not have known any of the daily tension and suffering recounted here.

I believe this to be a crucial truth to absorb: we suffer more acutely because we are Christians – and the more our Christian faith and hope energises our daily lives, the more we shall experience the intensity of this suffering.

This will become clearer as we walk with Paul through the experiences he describes in this passage.

It seems incredibly risky, if not foolish, to put priceless treasure in clay pots. Pots crack and crumble. God has deliberately chosen to store the glorious treasure of the gospel in very earthy and vulnerable human beings. He has no other place to put it. He knows very well that, like Paul, 'we are dust' (Ps. 103: 14); we have, not just feet of clay, but a constitution which is 'from the earth' (1 Cor. 15: 47). Quite simply, we are mortal; we crack up; we crumble; and, finally, we return to the dust (Gen. 3: 19).

A VERY EARTHEN VESSEL

Paul, probably well into his fifties when this letter was penned, was more conscious than most of his physical weakness: 'afflicted... perplexed... persecuted... struck down' are the words he uses to describe his regular life style (2 Cor. 4: 8-9). The poignant catalogues of personal suffering later in this letter (6: 4-10; 11: 23-9) serve to underline the battering, physical and emotional, which Paul seemed to undergo throughout his life as a Christian. He was indeed an 'earthen vessel', and he knew it. Denney comments: 'No one who saw the exceeding greatness of the power which the Gospel exercised... and looked at a preacher like Paul, could dream that the explanation lay in *him* – not in an ugly little Jew.'[1]

Here Paul is reminding us of an essential principle in the activity of God, which is effectively denied by those who proclaim a triumphalist gospel: the weaker the human vessel, the greater glory goes to God when lives are changed and manifest the presence of the Spirit.

I still remember (in the late 1960s) meeting Pastor Richard Wurmbrand, imprisoned for over fourteen years in Romanian gaols for his faith, often in solitary confinement and severely tortured in ways which were visibly impressed on his countenance. The man looked haggard, with sallow cheeks, pronounced rings under his eyes, the experience of pain within them, and a shuffling, unsteady gait. Those were his visible scars. But from this frail earthen vessel radiated the glory of the living God.

The strong, self-assured and successful often obscure the glory of God. Without such a contrast between human vulnerability and divine power, it is by no means clear when, and for what, God is responsible.

So, a primary aspect of what it means to experience death before life turns out to be this readiness to taste and reveal our weakness, 'to show that the transcendent power belongs to God and not to us' (4: 7). It is not natural for human beings to be unashamed of their weaknesses; it actually goes against the grain. Only if we have died – and continue to die daily – to our need to be visibly strong, will God begin to get glory in our lives. It is impossible for God and us to get the glory simultaneously.

Of course, this dying to self is possible only in identification with Jesus in his death and resurrection. By sinking our own desire for glory and honour with him, we are raised to a new life in the Spirit. For Paul this meant that 'while we live we are always being given up to death for Jesus' sake, so that the life of Jesus may be manifested in our mortal flesh' (4: 11). That has repercussions for everyone whom we touch in our daily lives – for Paul it meant life, for example, for the Corinthians (4: 12). Indeed, this death-into-life sequence so gripped Paul that he was renewed in his determination to press on with the daily tension of being a Christian because, 'as grace extends to more and more people, it will increase thanksgiving, to the glory of God' (4: 15). And if God gets the glory, says Paul, that is all that really matters.

With this description of what it means to have eternal treasure concealed, yet gloriously made available, in mere clay pots, Paul launches into a direct contrast between the suffering and the glory. He uses at least eight pairs of phrases to illustrate the contrast and we shall look at each pair in turn.

Our outer nature ... our inner nature (2 Cor. 4: 16). It is difficult to be sure precisely what Paul means by these two phrases, although the general meaning is obvious. Probably he has in mind roughly what he explained to the Corinthians earlier about being 'in Adam' and being 'in Christ'.[2] On that basis, 'our outer nature' (literally, 'the outside man') refers to everything I am as a created and sinful human being; 'our inner nature' (literally, 'the man inside') refers to all that I am in Christ as a reborn, redeemed child of God. The former is irretrievably wasting away, the latter is inexorably being renewed, i.e. kept fresh and vital.

This inner renewal is taking place 'day by day', not simply in special times of closeness to God when we feel that renewal in the Holy Spirit is taking place. God is at work in us to maintain this new life even when – especially when – we least feel like it. Such unseen, inner life is happening all the time in the created world around us: an obvious example is the chrysalis sloughing off its outer skin to reveal a butterfly.

Several years ago I had a very painful ingrown toe-nail, which had made the toe itself grow septic. It took a long time and specific prayer (but that is another story!) for the nail eventually to come free from the toe. Underneath was a perfectly-formed, though fragile, new toe-nail. It had been nurtured underneath the decaying old nail and came into its own only when the old nail could serve no further purpose, and when the new nail was ready for exposure to the outside world.

INEVITABLE TENSION

Both in creation and in re-creation, therefore, God is

working renewal into his creatures. But the renewing work of the Spirit is proceeding side by side with the decaying activity of the flesh. Because the two processes are necessarily intertwined within our mortal bodies, tension is inevitable. Because, also, what we are in Christ and what we are in Adam are not easily distinguishable in precise terms, we shall have to live with a considerable amount of ambiguity this side of heaven. Our bodies are wasting away and will return to the dust; but from time to time we shall know the healing and renewing work of God within our bodies, not just in their inbuilt ability to recover from sickness and damage, but in the direct intervention of God to bring immediate relief and healing.

However frequently or dramatically we experience healing in our mortal bodies – or however infrequently – we still have to come to terms with its 'bondage to decay'.[3] Although much concern today for physical health and fitness is greatly needed, the cult of youth and health is a glaring example of refusing to face up to the fact that 'our outer nature is wasting away'. In the same way, the reality and inevitability of death will help Christians in the medical profession to ask healthy questions about practices which seem to regard the death of a patient as the ultimate disaster and a professional failure. They would also find more space to break the conspiracy of silence or half-truths which sometimes surrounds the reality of terminal illness.

Affliction . . . glory (2 Cor. 4: 17). This verse epitomises the theme of the whole letter. It looks, superficially, like a mandate for playing down our earthly sufferings. Equally, on its own it could be taken as a sideswipe at any undue emphasis on glory here and now: it is clearly meant for later.

Neither interpretation does justice to either the content or the context of what Paul is saying. First, let us concede that for Paul there is absolutely no comparison between what he is going through now and what he will know ultimately in the glory of heaven. Whatever pressures he is undergoing, they are 'slight' and 'momentary' i.e. minimal in substance, significance and duration. He is given strength to press on precisely because he has felt the weight of glory with Christ.

But the force of Paul's statement in this verse is in the meaning of the verb, rather vapidly translated 'is preparing': 'this slight momentary affliction is preparing for us an eternal weight of glory beyond all comparison.' The word has the meaning of working something in at depth. It is used again a few verses later, when Paul says that God has been preparing us throughout our earthly lives for the fullness of eternal life in heaven (2 Cor. 5: 5). Now the significance of this perspective on our suffering is this: everything we experience that is difficult, painful and humbling is actually working the glory of God into us in the depths of our being.

One of my daughters recently had a very tough year. At the age of eleven, she had seven months or more of glandular fever. This was followed, immediately she had thrown it off, by a serious fracture of the upper arm. The net result, in terms which matter intensely to young people of her age, was losing most of a year's work and companionship at school – apart from several other painful and unpleasant experiences.

Looking back on this time of difficulty and suffering, we can see now that God used it all to work into her a noticeable shrewdness and sensitivity, as well as a stronger faith in Jesus. This shrewdness and sensitivity are intriguing in terms of the theme of glory, because we are told that the first disciples were privileged to see that glory in the life of Jesus: 'we beheld his glory, glory as of the only Son from the Father, full of grace and truth' (John 1: 14 AV). John seems to be saying: glory equals grace-plus-truth. In my daughter we have seen affliction working into her sensitivity (an aspect of grace) and shrewdness (an aspect of truth).

GLORY THROUGH SUFFERING

The glory, therefore, does not come in spite of the suffering; the glory comes in and through the suffering. Without the suffering there would be no glory; no cross, no crown.

'Suffering, for the Christian, is not an accident; it is a divine appointment and a divine opportunity.'[4]

It is not, therefore, only or mainly the fact of glory after death which makes our present affliction seem slight and momentary. In the middle of our affliction God is working the glory into us – and we are probably those least qualified to notice it. I am quite sure that the many elderly Christians, pressing on courageously with very fragile bodies, whom I have had the privilege of visiting and joining in prayer, are not in the least aware of the glory of the Lord which shines from within them.

The things that are seen... the things that are unseen (2 Cor. 4: 18). The first phrase refers to everything that is accessible to our senses, everything to do with the world around us as well as all that is mortal in us and about us. All this is 'transient', here for the moment and then gone. If we make these things the target of our gaze, we shall lose our nerve and find we have no heart for the path of discipleship. Paul remained of good courage and with buoyant spirits because he refused to concentrate on the evidence of his eyes and ears, of taste and touch.

We should, however, be misled if we deduced that, in the phrase 'the things that are unseen' which 'are eternal', Paul included only what he could not see, hear, smell, taste or handle. Central to his theological understanding was the perspective of two ages or two worlds: 'this age or world' and 'the age or world to come'.[5] In Jesus – in his birth and life, death and resurrection – the age/world to come has invaded this age/world. In him the kingdom of God has been manifested. Jesus reigns as Lord and his rule will one day be acknowledged openly by everyone. Everything the Bible teaches about the kingly rule of God in Jesus should become, therefore, the target for the Christian's concentration.

In the main, this overall reign of Jesus is unseen. If we fixed our eyes on what seems obvious all around us, whether our own mortality or the apparent supremacy of sin and evil or the spasmodic vitality of the Christian Church, we should soon be overwhelmed. Paul exhorts us, by his own example and teaching, to fix our attention on the things which are unseen, in that they reflect the character of the age/world to come (the literal meaning of the Greek word translated 'eternal'). Equally, those realities which are so oppressively dominant in our lives are transitory; their lifespan is severely limited – 'For all that is in the world, the lust of the flesh and the lust of the eyes and the pride of life, is not of the Father, but is of the world. And the world passes away, and the lust of it; but he who does the will of God abides for ever' (1 John 2: 16–17).

Earthly tent... a building... eternal (2 Cor. 5: 1). Paul is still looking hard and realistically at his own creaking and battered body. It is likely at any moment to reach its final dissolution (the force of the word 'destroyed' in v. 1). He is reminded of his own former trade as a tentmaker[6] and sees his body as a tent. However well-made, tents are designed for the pilgrim life. They are not intended for us to settle down in, and we must be ready to dismantle them, to strike camp, and to move on. This pilgrim spirit is necessary for our Christian lives all the way through this world; but it is supremely important when the time comes to leave it. Tents will be useless in the climate of heaven.

At the end of his own life Paul made it plain to the young man, Timothy, that he was ready to move on: 'the time of my departure has come. I have fought the good fight, I have finished the race, I have kept the faith' (2 Tim. 4: 6–7). In the same way, Peter saw his body as a tent and was able to face his own death with equanimity and poise: 'I think it right, as long as I am in this tent, to arouse you by way of reminder, since I know that the putting off of my tent will be soon, as our Lord Jesus Christ showed me' (2 Pet. 1: 13–14).

A HEAVENLY DWELLING

Paul contrasts the fragile vulnerable tent of his earthly body with the building which God has in store for him, 'a house not made with hands, eternal in the heavens.' Paul longs to put on this 'heavenly dwelling'. What exactly is he describing? It seems probable that he is looking forward to the new 'body' in which he, together with every Christian, will enjoy the fullness of eternal life in heaven.

He has already expanded on this theme at some length in his first letter to the Corinthians (1 Cor. 15: 35 ff.), where he talks about 'a spiritual body' into which as Christians we shall all be changed 'at the last trumpet.' At that climactic moment, 'the dead will be raised imperishable'. By his almighty, resurrection-power God will raise the dead in Christ and give them a spiritual body, perfectly fitted for the life of heaven, which Paul describes as imperishable, glorious, powerful and immortal – everything, in fact, which our earthly tent is patently not.

Yet, despite the total contrast between the earthly tent and the eternal building, there is continuity between them: without the first there cannot be the second, and the gift of the Holy Spirit to dwell within our earthly tent provides that link. Every experience of the Spirit's presence and power in our lives now is a guarantee and foretaste of our future fullness. That is why our experience of the Spirit now is inevitably paradoxical: we taste the reality of God and sense, rather than actually see, the glory of God. Yet these earthly bodies cannot cope with too much glory through the Spirit, and thus there is both a deeply satisfying and a thoroughly unsatisfying quality to even genuine experience of God here on earth. We long for more, but we cannot cope with too much.

Naked... clothed (2 Cor. 5: 3-4). At this stage Paul becomes more explicit about the tension inherent in being people of hope, people of the resurrection. He seems to refer to a very real fear that, between the uneasy familiarity of his earthly tent and the glorious fullness of his eternal building, he will 'be found naked.' This fear begins to make sense when we pause to take in Paul's understanding of death, and the way he sees it in relationship to the return of Jesus in glory – the parousia.

He eagerly looked forward to this return. He always hoped, though not always expected (particularly towards the end of his life), to be alive when it happened. He consistently sees death as falling asleep (1 Cor. 15: 51; 1 Thess. 4: 13 ff.; cf. John 11: 12). In his natural self he does not want to go through death, which he sees as being stripped and found naked – an experience of particular horror to Jews and, incidentally, one of the most powerful aspects of the crucifixion of Jesus, who through his nakedness exposed the power of darkness and the ghastly reality of sin.[7] Because of this fear, Paul would far rather not go through death, but simply at the parousia of Jesus receive his resurrection-body, and in this way be 'further clothed' without any intervening period of 'nakedness'.

FALLING ASLEEP

We need to stress that for Paul – and it is a fear which we probably all share – this shrinking from the actual experience of death was an eminently natural feeling: but it was only natural. On further reflection, this fear of what is seen as falling asleep need not paralyse or dominate us. Jesus has promised to come to each Christian at the point of death, and to take us to be with him where he is (John 14: 3). It appears that the Bible teaches that, at death, we fall asleep as Christians in Christ and with Christ;[8] and that our next conscious experience is on 'the last day' when, at the sound of 'the trumpet' (1 Cor. 15: 52) all believers together (i.e. those who have died down the centuries and those still alive at the time) will welcome the returning Jesus in glory, be given resurrection-bodies, and enter into the fullness of eternal life, 'and so we shall always be with the Lord' (1 Thess. 4: 17).

The language of sleep seems to me the most evocative and helpful, because it provides us with an analogy which we can appreciate without fully understanding what is going on. We fall asleep at night and, if we are fortunate, the next thing we know is waking up the next morning – or we assume it is the next morning on fairly good evidence (the sun, our watches, the radio, our appetites, the children's noise). But, to all intents and purposes, the passage of time has been (for us while asleep) virtually irrelevant: we have been unconscious; we do not have a clue what has been going on all the time we were asleep.

When, as Christians, we die, we fall asleep. Although we would, in our innate curiosity, like to know what goes on in this interim stage between the earthly tent and the eternal building, we do not know and we have no need to know. This creates an understandable fear of the unknown, but the Christian's confidence and peace are in Christ, and we fall asleep in him and with him. Why be afraid? I am sure that any lingering fears will be totally removed in that moment immediately before we die when Jesus himself comes to take us home, his home, where he has prepared a place specially for us.

I remember the death of a much-loved Christian in Cape Town several years ago. In the hospital bed, surrounded by his family, he had been motionless in a coma for over a fortnight. Nobody had been able to get through to him, and he had not communicated with his family in any way during those last days. He was surrounded with all the usual medical equipment. Suddenly he stretched out his arms and raised himself up from the bed; his face was transformed with a radiant smile, the smile of recognition and greeting. The moment was held for a second or so – and then he died. Nobody present was in any doubt that Jesus had come to take him to be with himself. So that Christian's last earthly experience was to be collected by his Saviour. Who can doubt that his next conscious experience is when he sees his Saviour's face in all his glory? We need not fear the nakedness.

What is mortal... life (2 Cor. 5: 4). In effect, this phrase summarises all that Paul has been saying. The force of its simplicity lies in its perspective on what real life means. One of the inherent tensions of being alive as Christians in this world is that, even when everything around us and within us is vibrant with joy and beauty, we know instinctively that it is all fleeting and extremely vulnerable. It only takes an earth tremor, a road accident, a cancer scare, or a reminder of nuclear explosion, to bring what we call life into the jaws of death.

The English word 'mortal' tends to obscure this harsh reality. It actually means riddled with death, taken from the Latin and no different from the mortuary. And yet Paul does not – here or elsewhere – write off every earthly experience as death-ridden. He uses a very picturesque and powerful word here when he says that what is mortal will be 'swallowed up by life.' The same word is used in the famous resurrection-passage in 1 Corinthians 15: 54, 'then shall come to pass the saying that is written, "Death is swallowed up in victory." ' So everything invaded by and touched by death, and death itself, will be absorbed into the victorious life of heaven. So death will be no more, and the sting of death has therefore already been drawn.

The picture of life swallowing up death is taken from a particularly vivid passage in Isaiah which is worth quoting in full:

. . . . the Lord of hosts will make for all peoples a feast of fat things, a feast of wine on the lees, of fat things full of marrow, of wine on the lees well refined. And he will destroy . . . the covering that is cast over all peoples, the veil that is spread over all nations. He will swallow up death for ever, and the Lord God will wipe away tears from all faces . . . It will be said on that day, 'Lo, this is our God; we have waited for him, that he might save us. This is the Lord; we have waited for him; let us be glad and rejoice in his salvation (Isa. 25: 6–9).

We have waited for him . . . and it is the long wait which is so difficult. The bigger and better the future, the harder the waiting. Children find waiting extremely difficult . . . and the children of God are no different.

Home . . . away (2 Cor. 5: 6–9). The tension of being a Christian in the world is no better seen than here. Paul sees us as either being at home in the body and away from the Lord, or at home with the Lord and away from the body. Most of the time we want to be *both* at home in the body *and* at home with the Lord. We want the best of both worlds all at once. This naivete leads to half-hearted discipleship, especially in the face of hardship and suffering. Much of the faulty teaching concerned with the subject of constant wealth, health and success is rooted in this false perspective: we can never be at home in the body, because it is not our home. The more we emphasise the good things of this life, the further we are moving away from the Lord.

Paul is, of course, not suggesting that the Lord is distant from us while we are in our earthly bodies – except in the sense that nothing in this life can conceivably compare with being for ever with the Lord in the perfection of heaven. Even those rare occasions when we feel so close to the Lord that we are standing on hallowed ground are not able to be compared with what we shall experience then, when we know even as we are known (1 Cor. 13: 12).

When you are living away from your true home for any
length of time, it is always good to receive different kinds
of reminders which keep alive the reality of home and
what it is like. When we were in Cape Town for nearly
eight years, it was always enjoyable to have visits, letters,
phone calls, presents, tapes, photographs, etc. Each one
underlined that our home was not so much South Africa as
England. There were many periods of ambivalence, when
away seemed like home. There were even some occasions,
on returning to England on leave, when home seemed like
away.

GOOD TO COME HOME

Paul has come to terms with living away from home all the
time, but he candidly wants to strike tent once and for all –
to get home. As the song puts it, 'It's nice to go travelling,
but it's so much nicer to come home.' The longer a
Christian has been on the road in this world, the more he
looks forward to coming home. It is not surprising,
therefore, that Christians who are still young do not
necessarily have such a ready expectancy. I remember
hoping against hope, as an upper teenager, that Jesus
would not return until I had been able to enjoy the good
things of this life, like marriage, travel and sporting
achievement (in no particular order!).

The longer we have been Christians the more we feel the
inherent tension in living away from home. Not only does
home usually seem so much closer and reachable, but the
sheer contrast with (often) the increasing weariness
involved in keeping on going in these earthly bodies
becomes almost too great. Paul expressed it in memorable
words: 'For to me to live is Christ, and to die is gain. If it is
to be life in the flesh, that means fruitful labour for me. Yet
which I shall choose I cannot tell. I am hard pressed

between the two. My desire is to depart and to be with
Christ, for that is far better. But to remain in the flesh is
more necessary on your account' (Phil. 1: 21-3).

You do not have to be a Christian minister of mature
experience, like Paul, to know this tension. Stress, pain,
illness, depression, failure or exhaustion can bring any
Christian to the same sense of constriction in a narrow
place.

We groan ... we sigh ... we are always of good courage (2
Cor. 5: 2, 4, 6). In this eloquent paradox Paul sums up the
impact on his own spirits of the previous seven contrasts.
It seems to me that this combination of groaning and
buoyancy is of the essence of Christian integrity and of
Christian discipleship. It is extremely hard to keep them
both in proper balance. This fact of Christian experience
reflects, I believe, the pattern of New Testament theology,
which is often one of apparently contrary truths which
need to be held in tension. The most obvious example –
and the one which tends to spill over into most other
aspects – is the sovereignty of God and the freedom of man.

The temptation, both in theology and in experience, is
to give undue prominence to one truth rather than the
other; or to emphasise first one truth and then the other; or
even deliberately to ignore one truth and to concentrate
exclusively on the other. This is happening frequently
today when some Christians ignore the groaning and the
sighing (even dismiss or condemn it) and constantly
emphasise the buoyancy.

We need to notice that the word 'groan' is not the same
as 'moan'. The Bible gives little room for moaning. The
word translated 'groan' is used of the Holy Spirit praying
within us with 'sighs too deep for words' (Rom. 8: 26), and
also of Jesus looking up to heaven and sighing deeply in
his spirit before releasing a deaf and dumb man to speak
clearly (Mark 7: 34). A clue to his depth of spiritual distress
is given in the saga of Lazarus' death, where we read twice

that Jesus was 'deeply moved' (John 11: 33, 38).

APPARENT FUTILITY

It seems unlikely that the predominant emotion in the heart of Jesus, when faced with the death of his friend, was one of grief – in the sense of mourning the loss of Lazarus. It seems to have been closer to an inner groaning of spirit in the face of the rampages of sin and death in God's creation. I remember an occasion about fifteen years ago, when I had been involved in ministry in the wake of the sudden death of an outstanding young Christian of twenty-seven. One afternoon not long after the funeral, I was sitting quietly at home recalling the events of the previous few days. I was gradually overcome with a profound inner groaning, accompanied by sobbing which shook my whole body through and through. The overriding sensation was not of particular grief at Michael's death but of general, but intense, sighing at the apparent futility and profound frailty of human life. I have had two or three similar experiences since that time.

Paul makes it clear that his own groaning is accentuated by his longing expectation for the fullness of eternal life in heaven. Indeed, if we do not have any faith or hope at all, we do not feel this groaning. In that very limited sense it is easier to live in this world as unbelievers. As I am writing this chapter, I am sitting at a table in a chalet in Switzerland. It is a beautifully warm and sunny day. I can see a glorious view of mountains and forests. But it is misty and the view is limited. I actually know that there are further mountain ranges in the distance which can add even greater grandeur to this panorama. If someone came here for the first time today, he would be thrilled and satisfied with the present vista. I am slightly frustrated by the partial view. I know it could be so much better and have sighed to myself several times this morning, 'I do wish the mist would clear.'

I hope, however, that my longing for a clearer, fuller view is not preventing any enjoyment of what is in front of my eyes. That is the temptation for Christians of a certain temperament, especially the perfectionist. Their very awareness of what might be eats away at their enjoyment of what is taking place. Paul, it seems, was able both to groan in the Spirit and maintain good courage at all times, even (or especially) when facing death – as he has been doing steadily and realistically in this passage.

* * *

One final comment is made by Paul in terms of his death: 'For we must all appear before the judgment seat of Christ' (2 Cor. 5: 10). As Denney comments: 'Many a time Paul has set himself in imagination in that great presence and let the awe of it descend upon his heart.'[9] No person has truly faced death unless he has likewise set himself in imagination in that great presence.

There may be, perhaps, an instinctive awareness of this 'eternity in man's heart' in the frank statement of Aldous Huxley: 'If you are a busy, film-going, newspaper-reading, football-watching, chocolate-eating modern, then death is hell.'

EQUANIMITY AND AWE

The Christian – and the Christian alone – can face death with both equanimity and awe. He need not be appalled by the prospect of being finally rejected, because his eternal destiny depends on the finished work of salvation accomplished by Jesus in his death and resurrection. But he will be filled with solemn awe at the searing scrutiny which will be applied to the whole of his life in Christ, down to its last detail, as the fire of God's truth tests 'what sort of work each one has done' (1 Cor. 3: 13). If it is good, i.e. like gold or silver or precious stones, it will receive a reward. If it is poor and worthless (the force of the word translated 'evil' – any connotation of moral corruption is misleading), i.e. like wood or hay or stubble, the Christian 'will suffer loss'; the loss of the work will not touch the person, because 'he himself will be saved' (1 Cor. 3: 15).

Perhaps we all need to create space to allow the fact of this scrutiny to impinge radically on our inner motives and daily lives. What ultimately matters in the light of this truth? In his grace the Lord will speak to us personally and powerfully, if we make such time for this crucial purpose. Those who are most busy in the Lord's service are probably in the greatest danger of perpetuating worthlessness. As Paul himself testifies, it is a question of whom we are aiming to please – ourselves, our family and friends, our congregation, or our Lord.

7

THE DEATH OF CHRIST

If facing the implications of our own death is one secret of holding together the twin realities of suffering and glory, the other secret is facing the implications of the death of Jesus. Much Christian discipleship today seems anaemic because the blood of Christ rarely receives the attention and understanding it requires. The very phrase, the blood of Christ, is offensive to some Christians and a sentimental cliché to others. Paul's teaching about the significance of Christ's death in the second part of chapter 5 is unique in its depth and power. It needs to be kept very carefully in its context.

The nub of the matter seems to lie in the famous verse: 'Therefore, if anyone is in Christ, he is a new creation; the old has passed away, behold, the new has come' (2 Cor. 5: 17). This was the favourite text of my first vicar: in just over four years I heard him preach on it three times, I believe. I am sure he is not alone in his love for the text. On reflection, however, the words have caused considerable confusion and frustration – not least when the text is used out of its context. This uncertainty has been put to me over the years with many variations, but overall there has been one theme: 'Exactly what has passed away? Precisely what new things have come in their place?'

There is considerable pathos in this question, because it

reflects the cry of the Christian heart. Glib answers only compound the problem. In fact, a particular reading of the Greek text also exaggerates the confusion. In the Revised Standard Version quoted above, there is no mention of the phrase 'all things'. These two words in the original could be taken either with the sentence at the end of v. 17: 'All things have become new',[1] or with the phrase at the beginning of verse 18: 'All this is from God...'[2]

A TOTAL TRANSFORMATION?

Those who take the first alternative tend to stress the complete revolution which takes place in those who have entrusted themselves to Christ, and are therefore 'in Christ'. Because, they say, Paul stresses that anyone in Christ is a new creation and that *all* things have become new, we can therefore expect a total transformation. The more sanguine and cautious urge patience. But the net result of insensitive and superficial teaching remains a flock of pastoral casualties: those who started out expecting (and expected) to become new people in Christ, but now find themselves burnt out and disillusioned because they seem to be very much the same as before, give or take a few religious exercises.

It is, of course, very possible to react to this teaching with such a low-level version of what it means to be in Christ that nothing much at all is expected by way of transformation. The only way out of this 'Catch 22' situation is through a more careful exposition of the whole passage in which Paul's great statement is found. The relevant passage (2 Cor. 5: 11–6: 2), as we have seen, has at its heart a profound understanding of the significance of Christ's death. The passing-away of the old and the ushering-in of the new can be legitimately interpreted only in such a context.

The determinative word in Paul's teaching about the

death of Christ is 'reconciliation'. The Greek word has the very simple connotation of making someone or something different. So Paul clearly wants the Corinthians to see that the basis of the change, brought about by being in Christ, resides in the event of the cross. God has done something utterly revolutionary in the death of his Son, and that alone can produce life-transforming change.

What precisely has God done in Jesus? We need to say straightaway that there is probably no single passage in the New Testament more acutely debated than 5: 18–21. 'This paragraph is one of the most pregnant, difficult and important in the whole of Pauline literature.'[3] With this caveat we shall take Paul's statements in order.

He begins with a succinct declaration, 'one has died for all' (5: 14). He repeats the statement twice in the following verse. The phrase in itself is not precise in its meaning: the very least it means is that Jesus died on behalf of all people. This is given more content by the clause: 'therefore all have died' – a phrase which introduces a powerful significance into the death of Jesus. He died on behalf of others in a way so effective that their own death is somehow included in his. Because he died in the way he did, others from that time onwards do not die in that way.

THE IMPACT OF SIN

How did Jesus die? What was involved for him in dying? Those questions Paul answers in verses 18–21. The answers explain the sense in which our own death does *not* involve what it involved for Jesus, and what our own death *would* have involved, were it not for his dying in that way. In verses 18–21 Paul makes it plain that the death of Jesus was bound up with our 'trespasses', with 'sin'. If there is any change in the human experience, and particularly the human experience of death, as a result of the death of Jesus, it is the impact of sin upon us.

In a word, before the death of Jesus God counted our trespasses against us. They were mounted high in our account before him. That created separation, alienation, enmity between us and God, in time and in eternity. Because it takes two to make and to break a relationship, it is not an exaggeration to say both that humanity was cut off from God by its sin, and that God was cut off from humanity by his holy rejection of sin. Every man and woman was, with accuracy and justice, regarded by God as a trespasser – falling short of his standards and walking all over his commandments.

There was, and still is, absolutely nothing that we could do about this situation of conflict. God took the initiative and 'through Christ reconciled us to himself.' Such was the pervasive infiltration of sin into human nature that God 'made him [Jesus] to be sin who knew no sin' (v. 21). That was the only way to demonstrate the eternal sinfulness of sin and to effect a radical change in men and women – radical enough to bring about a 'new creation' (v. 17). When Paul asserts that 'All this is from God' (v. 18), he is underlining the double-sided impact of the death of Jesus 'for our sake'. Our sin has been taken into Jesus in his dying and rising from the dead – and dealt with; God's holy anger with sin has been taken into Jesus in his dying and rising from the dead – and dealt with. As a result we, in Jesus, can become 'the righteousness of God' (v. 21).

RECEIVE THE GOOD NEWS

This is the good news of the Christian message: men and women are now urged to receive this good news – i.e. not to make peace with God, but to rejoice in the fact that in Christ Jesus God has made peace with the world. James Denney is at his most plain and persuasive in expounding this central message of the Gospel: 'Reconciliation is something God accomplished when, in the death of

Christ, he put away everything on his side that meant estrangement, so that he might come and preach peace ... The serious thing which makes the Gospel necessary, and the putting-away of which constitutes the Gospel, is God's condemnation of the world and its sin.'[4]

Some people would have us believe that at no time and in no sense did God sit in condemnation of the world, let alone that Jesus in his death propitiated an angry God. This latter assertion is, in any case, a parody of the teaching of the New Testament (setting up a man of straw in order to eradicate him and all his works). It is based on a rejection of certain elements of biblical truth because of a non-biblical view of God. This view essentially cannot conceive of anger, condemnation or judgment as consonant with the eternal love of God. God's love is thus interpreted, not on the basis of the entire biblical revelation, but on an eclectic use of certain passages, which are then set alongside human experiences of love.

Exponents of such a view, in its different forms, have always had the most extreme difficulty with verse 21. Typical of the comments is the following: 'St Paul's words here cannot be true, and yet it is possible that they are the best way of stating what is true.'[5] This remarkable double-talk is necessary only if we start from a position about God which has already rejected the truth stated in this particular verse.

Denney puts it baldly: 'God is love, they say, and therefore he does not require a propitiation. God is love, say the apostles, and therefore he provides a propitiation.'[6] He comments on this particular verse (5: 21): 'It is not the puzzle of the New Testament, but the ultimate solution of all puzzles.'[7]

It seems to be proper and essential gospel to affirm with Denney:

The wrath of God, the condemnation of God resting on the sinful world, are not ... unreal things, neither do they belong to ancient times. They are the most real things of which human nature has any knowledge till it receives the reconciliation ... It is the glory of the Gospel that it deals with them as real. It does not tell men they are illusions ... It tells them that God has dealt seriously with these things for their removal ... that God has made peace at an infinite cost, and that the priceless peace is now freely offered to them.[8]

GUILT BEFORE GOD

Denney is, I believe, particularly on target in describing humanity's inner experience of divine judgment in every culture and generation. When this sense of guilt before God is reduced by psychoanalysis into a dispensable subjective feeling, something intrinsically true is replaced by a damnable lie – and the fullness of our experience of God's salvation in Christ is diminished. If people are taught to believe that any sense of guilt before God is erroneous, they will be undisposed to receive the radically new relationship with God of which the gospel speaks so powerfully, not least in this part of 2 Corinthians.

Many Christians today live with no assurance of peace with God through the death of Jesus, not (as some would have us believe) because they have had guilt induced into them by a narrow creed, but because the eviscerated message passed on to them in the name of the Christian gospel has not begun to touch them in the core of their being – i.e. where, by God's common grace, God speaks to us all of our sinfulness, his holiness ... and the total revolution made possible between us and him through the death of his Son for our sake. For such people there has been little or no experience of this new relationship, because they were told no such new relationship was necessary. How can there be, in this kind of situation, any expectation (let alone experience) of inner change and reconciliation with God? Pascal put it with characteristic clarity: 'It is equally dangerous for man to know God without knowing his own wretchedness, as to know his own wretchedness without knowing the Redeemer who can cure him.'[9]

What has happened today is a slow and subtle shifting of the grounds for Christian experience away from all that God has done in Christ to whatever I may feel or do with God's help. Change becomes my responsibility, not God's gracious application by his Spirit of Christ's finished work on the cross. No wonder I meet Christian teachers – of pessimistic bent and disillusioned spirit – exhorting those entrusted to their care not to expect inner change. Who can cope with verse 17 of 2 Corinthians 5 without the glory of verses 18–21?

A MATTER OF EXPECTATIONS

Pastorally, it is a matter of expectations. On the practical level it boils down to whether we are prepared to sit down with people and pray with them for change. I was speaking with a colleague about summer ministry with teenagers. The particular work with which she is involved has a high leader-to-teenager ratio, with the intention that there should be thorough one-to-one care. She was expressing considerable concern that experienced leaders were not spending time in prayer with young people who raised personal needs and problems. I find myself wondering why there should be such reluctance. Is it because in prayer we are actually recognising God's presence and inviting him to do something to change things and people, particularly people? Can that constitute a threat to our own unwillingness to be changed? I certainly know this tendency to hold back in my own heart and, therefore, ministry.

God has, then, introduced us in Christ into a totally new relationship with himself. We have peace with God. He is our Father, from whom we can never be separated. The old reality of separation and alienation is finished. Our sin has been dealt with. God's hostility has been dealt with. The situation between God and mankind has been fundamentally and eternally changed. There is true reconciliation. Death will not alter this new relationship: it will in fact open the way to its fulfilment. The way Jesus died – experiencing separation from God because, in being made sin, he was exposed to God's judgment on sin – is no longer the way those who are in Jesus die.

We are now in a better position to return to the cry of the Christian heart: 'What old things have passed away? What new things have arrived?' In brief, the answer is that a totally new relationship with God has been created. The implications of this relationship become apparent as we look more closely at the surrounding verses.

The first and most striking point to emerge is that Paul is describing personal relationships in every direction. So we can say immediately that, for Paul, the significance of his totally new relationship with God lies in transformed relationships across the board. He states unequivocally that 'From now on, we regard no one according to the flesh' (2 Cor. 5: 16). Paul recognises the fundamental truth that he is no longer 'in the flesh', but 'in the Spirit'[10] – and he has decided to relate to others accordingly.

Paul appears to have in mind his pre-conversion life as a Pharisee. Although this is never explicitly mentioned in this passage, he is clearly recalling what he used to be like before he came to know God in Jesus Christ. The most absorbing influence in those days was his adherence to the party of the Pharisees.[11] His formidable opponents at Corinth were self-conscious Judaisers, who would have forcibly reminded Paul of Saul the Pharisee (2 Cor. 11: 22). He is, therefore, at pains now to emphasise the inner revolution brought about by his conversion. We shall see that he constantly makes implicit contrasts with the way Pharisees behave.

In taking his stand on the new creation which God has

made him in Christ, Paul outlines several inner drives – all
derived from 'the flesh' – which no longer dictate to him.
They are all part of the 'old things' which have 'passed
away'.

1. The need to cover up (5: 11). It is natural for us to cover
up what we are really like, because we are terrified of what
might happen if people see us as we really are. As a
Pharisee, Paul used to be governed by this need: Jesus had
laid bare the true nature of the Pharisees' inner hearts
when he declared: 'you are like whitewashed tombs, which
outwardly appear beautiful, but within they are full of
dead men's bones and all uncleanness. So you also
outwardly appear righteous to men, but within you are
full of hypocrisy and iniquity' (Matt. 23: 27–8).

Paul had been set free from this powerful bondage:
'what we are is known to God' and makes no difference to
his acceptance of us in Christ. If God, who knows me as I
really am, has said an unequivocal 'Yes' to me in Jesus,
then I have no longer any need to cover up what I am like.
In an intriguing word play with the previous verse, Paul
stresses that what he is before God and the Corinthians is
abundantly plain and in the open – just as it will be 'before
the judgment seat of Christ'. In other words, Paul is now
entirely open with everyone, because that is what it will be
like then. He allows the reality of that great day to
determine his transparency in personal relationships.

2. The need to impress others (5: 12). Paul wrestles
throughout this letter with the temptation to establish his
own reputation in the eyes of the Corinthians. The
number and the virulence of his detractors constantly
lured him to do something which he hated – in chapter 11
of the letter he gives in to the temptation, so extreme is the
pressure. But in fact Paul regards this insatiable need to
commend himself as part of the old nature which in Christ
has been dealt with and passed away.

Like Paul, we all like people to think well of us. We need only to test ourselves when we meet others for the first time. It is very difficult, as well as letting them know who we are, not to let them know a little of what we have done. Our identity is so easily wrapped up in our achievements or position. Paul specifically refers to 'those who pride themselves on a man's position and not on his heart.' Although Pharisees epitomised this attitude, always seeking to impress others with their piety and importance,[12] it is deeply ingrained into human nature. It is easy to be impressed by – and to seek to impress others with – such things as clothes, accent, education, articulacy, status, contacts, or reputation.

In Christ Paul has discovered the freedom of a conscience free before God and open with his fellows. Such freedom is far more to be prized than any combination of impressive externals we could muster. However tentative his grasp on this inner freedom might have been at times, especially under pressure from Corinthian opponents, Paul saw it as intrinsic to his new life in Christ.

3. The need to control himself (5: 13–15). 'For if we are beside ourselves, it is for God; if we are in our right minds, it is for you. For the love of Christ controls us'. In this fascinating statement, Paul probably means that there were two essential ingredients in his ministry – the non-rational and the rational. To appreciate the importance of this we need to take a closer look, especially at the first sentence.

The Greek word translated 'we are beside ourselves' provides the root for the English word 'ecstasy'. Without bothering too much about nuances of interpretation, we can safely assume that Paul is referring to his own experience of the Spirit's work within him in ways which bypassed the mind. We know that such supra-rational experience was common and highly valued at Corinth.

Paul has spent three chapters in his first letter writing about abuses and misunderstandings concerning such matters (1 Cor. 12–14). In spite of excesses he has steadily refused to be driven into a cynical or dismissive attitude. In this terse statement, therefore, he is asserting the total legitimacy of such experiences: they are 'for God'.

That statement is not a refusal to have such experiences subjected to any scrutiny whatever. Paul's guarantee of their authenticity is in the fact that he is controlled by the love of Christ. He has reached a sober conviction that his life, rational or non-rational, is no longer his own: it belongs to Jesus Christ, because he died and was raised for all people, including Paul. His non-rational experience is not, therefore, a personal indulgence or a remnant of pietistic escapism. On the contrary, it represents Paul's complete submission of himself as a whole person to the Lord out of gratitude for his immense love for him. As he thus presents himself to the Lord, the Lord meets him in ways which bypass his mind.[13] It seems more than likely that Paul is referring to specific ways in which the Holy Spirit interacts with his human spirit, for example through speaking with tongues and through visions.[14]

RELENTLESS SELF-CONTROL

Such non-rational experience of God requires in any Christian the readiness to release to God that relentless self-control which we maintain so carefully, especially if we are trained to think logically about everything and to keep a tight rein on our emotions with our clear minds. I know all too well how easy it is to exercise a rigid mental censorship over my own relationship with God. In Christian ministry I find it very difficult to see things and people getting out of control. The last thing I choose to do is to get into any situation where I am not in control.

Paul, on the other hand, is clear about the source of

control in his life: it is the love of Christ, not his own mind. Nevertheless, Paul remains adamant that his ministry equally includes the rational and the non-rational. His mighty intellect, redeemed and put to use for the glory of God, has been at work teaching and unfolding the wealth of God in Jesus Christ. He has made these gifts available through God for the benefit of the Corinthians: 'if we are in our right mind, it is for you.' Again, the controlling power in this essential aspect of his ministry is the love of Christ, which ensures that his teaching and preaching are for the sake of others, including the Corinthians, and not for self-satisfaction or even self-fulfilment.

So, whether in the non-rational or the rational aspects of his ministry, Paul had lost the need to keep himself controlled – a particular mark in the steely discipline which Pharisees imposed upon themselves. He had someone greater controlling him – Christ. That was the inner revolution which had made Paul a new creature altogether. In Christ he was free from the need to live for himself, especially in the subtle way involved when we allow anything but the love of Christ to control us.

4. *The need to assess others* (5: 16). We probably all know the experience of being weighed up by someone, not just at first encounter, but as a habit. There are those who always seem to be putting through a sieve those with whom they live and work – assessing, sifting, evaluating, forming judgments. Such people seem to have well-defined pigeon-holes into which they slot all and sundry. The criteria they use are sometimes purely external, based on outward appearances. But often they make their assessment of others on the basis of personal intuition, instinct or convenience. People are seen in terms of their productivity or their personal attractiveness or their particular talents, not as individuals created in the image of God and therefore to be accepted and loved in Christ.

In the film *The Elephant Man*, John Hurt plays the part of John Merrick, a person grotesquely deformed from birth, who is rescued from the role of a freak being paraded to the public in local fairs by the concern of a London physician, Dr Treaves. In one of the most powerful scenes in the film, the deformed man is being chased by a curious and hostile mob into the public toilets at Victoria Station. As he is surrounded like a caged animal, he shouts out, 'I'm a person, I'm a person,' before collapsing on the ground groaning, 'I'm a man, a man.' The whole film dramatically presents the trauma facing John Merrick as he discovers his personhood through the care of Dr Treaves – *and* the trauma experienced by all those who meet such a deformed person. Just before he dies, he exclaims with spontaneous joy: 'I feel very happy. I enjoy each moment of every day to the full, because I know I am loved' – arguably one of the best descriptions we have anywhere of the impact of the gospel on one man's life.

I suppose one of the reasons why we all have this natural tendency to categorise people is the sense of comfortable safety it engenders: safety from the raw challenge of meeting and relating to people as they are, instead of what we would like them to be; safety, also, from the costly business of letting others meet and relate to us as we really are.

PRECONCEIVED CATEGORIES

Paul readily admits that he used to assess people in this kind of way, 'according to the flesh' and 'from a human point of view'. As a result of being made a new creature in Christ he has stopped doing it, because the need has been taken away. Indeed, Paul recognises that he used to take up a purely human and fleshly attitude to Jesus Christ himself – presumably basing his estimate on the information he had gleaned and fitting Jesus into the preconceived categories of Pharisaism. On this basis Paul had been able to dismiss the claims of Jesus to be the Messiah and had been, in all good conscience, perfectly happy to persecute to death those who became his followers. When God broke into his life, shining the light of the gospel into his inner being on the road to Damascus, Paul began to see Christ in a completely new way.

In his intense encounter with the Jews, especially the Pharisees, during his own earthly ministry, Jesus had to confront his opponents with the highly-limited perspective from which they were looking so dismissively at him. The crux of this confrontation is contained in the following conversation:

Again Jesus spoke to them, saying, 'I am the light of the world; he who follows me will not walk in darkness, but will have the light of life.' The Pharisees then said to him, 'You are bearing witness to yourself; your testimony is not true.' Jesus answered, 'Even if I do bear witness to myself, my testimony is true, for I know whence I have come and whither I am going, but you do not know whence I come or whither I am going. You judge according to the flesh, I judge no one' (John 8: 12–15).

It was typical, therefore, of the Pharisees to be constantly assessing everyone, Jesus included, from a purely human point of view, 'according to the flesh'. Until a person knows the inner transformation of being reborn by God's Spirit, he remains bound by and bound to such assessments of people, including Jesus.

These inner drives of our unredeemed human nature are among the old things which have passed away for those, like Paul, who are now in Christ. They have been drained of their irresistible power through the inner revolution made possible by the death of Christ and made real by the Spirit of the living God. In their place is a freedom towards

God as beloved children with their Father, and freedom towards others in the love of Christ. 'All this is from God' (2 Cor. 5: 18). As we experience it more and more, so we experience both the suffering and the glory.

8

EVANGELISM

In the next five chapters we shall look at five key themes all of which derive from the teaching which Paul has jus given on the significance of the death of Christ fo; becoming new creatures in Christ. I believe that these five themes (and there are probably others) are of major importance in an authentic discipleship which embraces both the suffering and the glory of being Christians. The five themes are: evangelism (2 Cor. 5: 18–6: 10), holiness (6: 14–7: 1), space in relationships (6: 11–13 and 7: 2–4), repentance (7: 5–16), and generosity (8: 1–9: 15).

I have no intention of adding to the plethora of books on the subject of evangelism. My purpose in this chapter is to show, within the compass of Paul's own experience and insights, how evangelism becomes the heart-beat of those who have been made new creatures in Christ, and that such a life style involves both suffering and glory. It may, again, be unwillingness to face suffering in various forms which is the biggest obstacle to evangelism in the Church today.

Having said this, I must hasten to add that there seems to be a turn of the tide in the Church in Britain in the matter of discipleship and evangelism. In 1977, on a visit to England from South Africa, I came across a widespread pessimism, if not depression, among most Christians I met. This included those who, a decade earlier, had been in the forefront of a quietly confident, if not buoyant, proclamation of the gospel. Ten years or more of coping with sniping and undermining opposition from those uncommitted to and cynical about biblically-based evangelism had taken its inevitably painful toll.

A NEW CONFIDENCE

The scene is very different towards the end of 1984. There is a new confidence, a growing expectancy, a more rounded testimony, a more imaginative boldness. I think there is also a more realistic appreciation of the cost of faithful evangelism, coupled with a resolute determination to walk the necessary road. Evangelism in its fullness (as described by Paul in the passage from 2 Cor. 5: 18 to 6: 10) is a way of life, a front-line confrontation with all that is opposed to Jesus Christ and his gospel. For a long time it has seemed clear to me that a new and deeper experience of God's Spirit is inextricably tied up with fresh initiatives in and readiness for evangelism. Equally, we shall enter into a greater experience of the various gifts of the Spirit only as we launch out together in evangelism. The gifts of the Spirit are weapons of warfare, not lovely presents for Christians on vacation. That much is abundantly clear from the catalogue of Paul's experiences as an ambassador for Christ in 6: 4–10.

For too long many Christians have indulged in the effete luxury of debating the pros and cons of certain gifts of the Spirit in an intellectual vacuum, assuming that truth in spiritual matters is to be discovered in discussion and at conferences. A full-orbed evangelism in the power of the Spirit can be discovered only in the cut and thrust of direct encounter with the opposition, whatever it happens to be – and it is everywhere.

One of the saddest facts about much local church life is

its non-involvement in this direct encounter. Where in recent years there has been most talk – and often outward evidence – of spiritual life, there has been little or no consistent involvement in evangelism. Congregations have sprung up which consist of disaffected members of existing churches, with scarcely anyone having been converted from paganism and unbelief. In such fellowship the glory is somewhat tarnished because it is second-hand: everything looks good but feels wrong. Church life has been turned into a comfortable ghetto, instead of being an army on the move.

AN AMBASSADOR FOR CHRIST

Paul's description of his own life and ministry provides an urgent corrective to any such tendencies. To state the obvious, his ministry as an ambassador for Christ springs directly from his encounter with Christ and his experience of Christ's power to change him. For Paul this experience was a day-to-day exposure to the power of the Spirit, 'being changed into his likeness from one degree of glory to another' (2 Cor. 3: 18). He sees himself as a messenger of change, of a totally altered situation between God and human beings: 'the old has passed away, behold, the new has come' (5: 17). On the basis of this new vocation as Christ's ambassador Paul gets down on his knees to beseech men and women to accept the reconciliation with God which God has provided through his Son's death.

There is a remarkable contrast between Paul's calling to be Christ's ambassador and his willingness to plead with men and women to be reconciled to God. Ambassadors do not humiliate themselves by beseeching people to change their minds. As Denney puts it, 'The ambassador as a rule stands upon his dignity; he maintains the greatness of the person whom he represents.'[1] Britons would not expect their ambassador in Tripoli or Moscow or Washington to descend to entreaty in the face of provocation, hostility or outrage. Libyan, Russian or American ambassadors would not behave in that way in London. Yet Paul, as ambassador for the King of kings, was prepared to plead with anyone and everyone to be reconciled to God: 'He is conscious of the grandeur of his calling, yet there is nothing that he would not do to win men to his message.'[2]

This paradoxical combination of being gripped by the awesome greatness of our calling and at the same time unashamedly pleading with people to come back to God seems to be the core of biblical evangelism. In fact Jesus himself combined the two truths in his own mission: it was in humbling himself that he proclaimed the message of reconciliation. For him the message lay as much in the nature of his mission as in the words he proclaimed. Marshall McLuhan popularised the catch-phrase: the medium is the message. With Jesus, his ministry was his message. Any faithful ambassador of Jesus will, therefore, have a similarly double theme – and Paul explicitly asserts that he has received from God both 'the ministry of reconciliation' (5: 18) and 'the message of reconciliation' (5: 19).

LIFE STYLE AND TESTIMONY

If we take both those words seriously – ministry and message – we shall examine more closely the daily life style which we are following as individual Christians and in our local churches. In these two contexts are we living as servants (the meaning of the word 'minister') and is the good news on our lips? Do both our behaviour and our testimony point to reconciliation between God and people? Are we prepared to humble ourselves before others in order to urge upon them the need to be reconciled to God?

We can ask the questions another way. Do we accept our

calling to be ambassadors for Christ? Does our life style illuminate the radical difference between the country whose king we serve and the country in which we are temporarily residing as 'strangers and exiles' (Heb. 11: 13)? There are few places more British than the expatriate British community overseas (especially in and around the embassy). The costly character of such distinctive living will be highlighted in the next chapter on holiness. For the present, we need honestly to ask ourselves whether we are not standing on some assumed dignity, in often not being prepared to beseech and plead with people directly to be reconcilied to God. For Paul it was a matter of consummate urgency: 'Behold, now is the acceptable time; behold, now is the day of salvation' (2 Cor. 6: 2).

So far, Paul's emphasis on evangelism has challenged us on at least four levels: our own experience of inner change, our acceptance of our calling as Christ's ambassadors, our life style as servants on the frontiers in enemy-occupied territory, and our sense of urgency about the opportunities presented by today. In 6: 3–10 Paul describes what this will inevitably mean. We will see that most of the things he itemises run directly against the grain of our personal likes and comforts. But these are priorities if massive obstacles are not going to be placed in the way of those who are hungry to know God. These three costly priorities are: endurance under pressure (vv. 4, 5), consistency in behaviour (6, 7), and acceptance of paradox (8–10).

1. ENDURANCE UNDER PRESSURE (6: 4, 5). The words translated 'through great endurance' seem to be the prelude to what follows: endurance is needed in all the situations mentioned in these two verses. Paul gives a list of nine things for which he has found it necessary to practise endurance. The literal meaning of 'endurance' is 'waiting underneath'. Such patient waiting is important for those who are seeking both to commend God and to be

commended by God in their daily lives. The nine things come in three groups of three and reveal differing causes of pressure on Christians committed to evangelism as a way of life.

(a) Pressure through inevitable circumstances. Taking each word in its literal meaning, we discover that 'afflictions' refers to situations which rub or grate; 'hardships' covers anything which we simply cannot avoid; 'calamities' means narrow places where we feel hemmed in. Any Christian committed to evangelism will find himself pressurised by such circumstances. Evangelism, if it is to bring glory to God and glory to our inner being, will not be smooth, attractive or trouble-free. It will bring us into all kinds of painful and awkward situations. People will wear us down by continual harassment. We will find ourselves in places where we wish we could run away, but where there is no way back and no detour. There is no choice but to press ahead through the flak.

We are called to stay firm and steady under such pressure. This goes against a common contemporary cliché, which asserts that if God is in it everything will fall into place. In certain (rather rare, I would suspect) circumstances – perhaps linked more to personal guidance than to active service as Christ's ambassadors day by day – God does indicate his presence and blessing by smoothing the path before us. More normally, however, the road is not smooth or easy – as Jesus himself explicitly warned.[3] If God is in what we are doing, there will be a good deal of affliction, hardship and calamity. Are we prepared to hold in there underneath all those things, not rebelling or moaning?

At its heart, this tendency to call off our involvement in a situation of opportunity and challenge can be nothing less than a relatively unsubtle rebelliousness. We do not like the way things are turning out; we cannot face the cost of pressing on; and so we rationalise both what is happening and the way we are reacting, and we say, 'God is clearly not in this, because it is not working out.' One wonders how many evangelistic opportunities have been cast aside because, just at the very moment when endurance was required, we have lost our nerve and walked out of the battlefield.

We probably do not realise how much we are all children of the instant generation. It is very humbling to read of and to meet Christians who have stayed for many years on the frontiers of evangelistic engagement in extremely vulnerable situations – often isolated, unappreciated, unrecognised and misunderstood. Such people have set their faces against the need for results and for difficulties to be removed.

(b) Pressure through specific opposition. The three words used next by Paul together paint a picture of a man subjected to intense physical, mental and emotional battering. The first word refers to physical beatings, the second to being kept forcibly locked up or severely restricted in his movements, and the third covers what was perhaps as unpleasant as anything he faced – uncontrollable people or situations where his life was in peril because of the evil powers unleashed by opposition forces.

Paul faced this kind of ordeal in several cities. In the Acts of the Apostles Luke records such experiences in at least eight cities – Antioch, Iconium, Lystra, Philippi, Thessalonica, Corinth, Ephesus and Jerusalem. The man was constantly under pressure from direct opposition *because* he was committed to the ministry and message of reconciliation as Christ's ambassador. In different parts of the world – and not just in the obvious places – such a commitment still produces the same opposition.

A young man in his early twenties was recently visiting a particular house in his parish on one of the most depressed estates in Huddersfield. When he knocked on the door, it was opened by the man of the house. 'What do you want?' he demanded. 'I want to speak to your wife about Jesus,' the young man replied – and immediately received a hefty kick on his shins and was told to get out. The Christian's reaction? 'I'm going back to the house to talk to that guy about Jesus.'

It is not at all pleasant to be attacked by people who, either because of alcohol or other drugs or demonic control, suddenly launch into an unexpected assault on you because you are an ambassador for Christ. I remember a colleague being treated like this more than once in his commitment to an evangelism which did not falter, let alone give up, when the opposition was at its fiercest. On one occasion, I was similarly threatened with a metal chair by a man just released from prison after serving time for assault and battery. I had just watched him high on glue, hurl tables, chairs, crockery and cutlery across the room, and I had no reason to suspect that he would not carry out his more personal threat on me. Actually he didn't and, because I am a coward in the face of physical violence, I was mightily relieved.

Paul – and countless Christians ever since – have endured patiently under such pressure. A consistent evangelistic life style will face similar treatment. The opposition – so far from suggesting that God is not in the situation – actually confirms that he is in it, and it is precisely that fact which provokes the opposition.

(c) Pressure through personal choice. You would have to be something of a masochist, with an element of the martyr-complex, to choose even more pressure than that brought about through inevitable circumstances and through specific opposition. Yet Paul is clear, in his next three words, that he has deliberately chosen a life style involving further hardship in order to be more convincing as an ambassador of Christ. The three words are 'labours, watching, hunger'. The last two refer to going without sleep and food. In their normal usage in the New

Testament they actually describe specifically fasting and staying awake for more effective ministry, but especially in order to pray. Paul is probably referring to his own discipline of making special times for prayer in preference to normal habits of eating and drinking.[4]

The word for 'labours' is the one he uses to describe every Christian's authentic life in Christ: 'Therefore, my beloved brethren, be steadfast, immovable, always abounding in the work of the Lord, knowing that in the Lord your labour is not in vain' (1 Cor. 15: 58). It is 'almost a technical word for Christian work',[5] and Paul refers to his own labour among the Christians at Thessalonica in the same way (1 Thess. 3: 5).

It is surely a timely reminder in today's mood, to note Paul's deliberate choice of a life style which cut across the dictates of personal comforts and desires. As an ambassador he could not please himself. I know myself how easy it is to fall into the equal and opposite trap of becoming a workaholic – labouring flat out not by personal choice to commend the Lord, but out of an inner driven-ness which cannot stop and is often self-justification. But Paul's example stresses that an evangelistic life style is sheer hard slog, means saying a continuous 'No' to ourselves, and will often mean cutting out what others regard as normal and their right.

It is one thing to have spasmodic bouts of hard slog in Christian discipleship. Paul writes about his steady endurance over several years. It is his chosen manner of life, because it is consistent both with the importance of his calling and with the urgency of the situation.

2. CONSISTENCY IN BEHAVIOUR (6: 6, 7). We are all conscious of inner contradictions in our behaviour, and we know that they do not commend the Lord. People always jump on the failures and misdemeanours of those who are known to be ambassadors of Christ. One of the strange facts in human nature is that the most out-and-out unbeliever has

an almost instinctive sense of the way Christians ought to behave. If as Christians we are committed to an evangelistic life style in the front line, we shall be under the most critical scrutiny. Because we are so much in the public eye in this sense, it is good to see what marks of Christian discipleship Paul regards as priorities.

There seem to be five combinations in these verses, each of which strikingly commends the gospel. The first two words, purity and knowledge, join together what we cannot ever afford to put asunder – i.e. inner holiness and knowledge about God. If there is any divorce between the two, the evangelistic impact is blunted, if not effectively reversed. When such inner contradiction becomes known, arguably more damage is done than any positive results of effective preaching or personal testimony.

The second combination to which Paul bears witness is between gentleness and power: 'forbearance, kindness ... the power of God'. The illusion that God's power is seen in dramatic, up-front, overwhelming ways is shattered only with great difficulty. If our estimate is correct, Paul had to unlearn attitudes to power which he had been taught over the years. He also had to learn how to let the Spirit of God deal with his impatience and write into him the character of Christ. Big-heartedness and gentle kindness did not come naturally to Saul of Tarsus. At first, he did not see these qualities as true strength: God had to create them within him. An ambassador for Christ is precisely that: not simply talking about Christ, but increasingly demonstrating the character of Christ.

Equally, Paul stresses the combination of 'genuine love' and 'truthful speech'. Such a combination is a priceless possession and gives probably more conviction to evangelism than anything else. It is a rare combination: those strong on truthful speech are often weak on genuine love; those who emphasise the primacy of love sometimes end up being very mealy-mouthed when truthful speaking is required. Again, it is in Jesus that we see such grace and truth perfectly personified. As his ambassadors we dishonour him when we fail to hold love and truth together.

LOVE AND TRUTH

Today I received a letter from overseas with a friend's remarks about the life of a particular church. Without commenting on either the accuracy or the appropriateness of his perception, I quote the words he uses to describe what he sees: '...Love which is all charm, friendly and gracious; the absence of truth and frank honesty – the lack of coping with real situations and the real world, the absence of courage to tackle the thorny problems.' He goes on to refer to 'a number of folk for whom religion or their faith is an escape from reality.' Among other things, these comments articulate the cry of the human heart for the love and truth to be found only in Jesus, but by his Spirit also in those called to be his ambassadors.

Paul's fourth combination is between active righteousness and the Holy Spirit. I stress this because both have been super-spiritualised. Righteousness is interpreted solely in terms of a person's new relationship with God through his justification of the sinner because of the atoning death of Jesus; the Holy Spirit's work is seen as something which takes place when I 'let go and let God'. The biblical record holds together the Christian's disciplined commitment to active righteousness of all kinds and the powerful ministry of the Holy Spirit.

Thus, those who are concerned to see righteousness prevail in the world at all levels can go nowhere without the inner resources of the Holy Spirit. Equally, when people are filled with the Holy Spirit, the evidence will be seen in active righteousness of all kinds. One of the saddest divisions of the last fifty years or so has been between social gospellers and hot gospellers. There is encouraging evidence, in Britain at least, of Christians from both traditions coming together 'with the weapons of righteousness for the right hand and for the left', and explicitly recognising the need for the power of the Holy Spirit. Only in this way will the Church maintain an authentic witness as ambassadors for Christ.

Lastly, Paul maintains such consistent behaviour whatever the climate of public opinion and regardless of what people think about or do to him – 'in honour and dishonour, in ill repute and good repute.' After his previous remarks this sounds a relatively harmless statement. In fact, it is extremely hard to maintain consistent behaviour throughout the fluctuating moods and whims of onlookers. When the atmosphere is favourable, it is tempting to drop our guard. When it is hostile, it is easy to resort to self-justification or retorting to criticism with criticism.

3. ACCEPTANCE OF PARADOX (6: 8-10). Paul has already hinted at the paradox at the heart of Christian discipleship in his treatment of the twin themes of suffering and glory. The two do not sit naturally together in human reasoning. In this passage he states the inherent paradox of Christian experience in the world. It is superbly expressed in the New English Bible:

> ... we are the impostors who speak the truth; the unknown men whom all men know; dying we still live on; disciplined by suffering, we are not done to death; in our sorrows we always have cause for joy; poor ourselves, we bring wealth to many; penniless, we own the world.

NO TIDY ANSWERS

There is fundamental tension involved in living with

paradox. We prefer to have tidy answers to life's problems, so that everything is neatly and easily explained. For example, it would be much less complicated if all suffering could be traced in a straight line from one person's sin to his suffering. Again, it would be simple if all those who put Jesus Christ first in their lives were obviously blessed materially. Because we instinctively want explanations of what we cannot understand, we can easily blind ourselves to the painful and mysterious elements of Christian discipleship – encapsulated in the words written above, 'unknown ... dying ... disciplined .. poor ... penniless'. Through those experiences we come to know true wealth and make many others wealthy. To the extent at which we balk at this paradox, to that extent we are less convincing as ambassadors for Christ.

Unbelievers are often looking desperately for such integrity and reality in Christians. Unfortunately, we think they are looking for answers to, if not the removal of, their problems. The Lord is not the answer to people's problems: he is God almighty and, in his grace and truth, wants everyone to know his love in forgiveness of their sins and in the free gift of his Spirit. That is the ministry of reconciliation which he has entrusted to all those who have become new creatures in Christ.

Pascal, the seventeenth-century French thinker and mathematician, expressed the core of Christian paradox most vividly in his *Pensées*. He saw man himself as a paradox:

What sort of freak then is man! How novel, how monstrous, how chaotic, how paradoxical, how prodigious! Judge of all things, feeble earthworm, repository of truth, sink of doubt and error, glory and refuse of the universe! ... Know then, proud man, what a paradox you are to yourself ... Learn that man infinitely transcends man, hear from your master your true condition, which is unknown to you. Listen to God.

From this beginning Pascal describes other essential paradoxes: 'Faith embraces many apparently contradictory truths... The origin of this is the union of two natures in Christ. And also the two worlds. The creation of a new heaven and a new earth. New life, new death. Everything duplicated and the same names remaining.' This paradox is true of Christians, says Pascal: 'All the names fit them: righteous sinners; living dead; dead living; reprobate elect, etc.'

But the ultimate paradox, which gives both rise to and reason for the Christian's constant experience of paradox in daily discipleship, lies right here: 'A God humiliated even to death on the Cross... A Messiah triumphing over death by his death.'[6]

9

HOLINESS

Not so long ago the congregation of St Aldate's in Oxford took a thorough look at the strengths and weaknesses of its life and witness. This examination covered a period of about three months and every attempt was made to give as many people as possible the chance to express their opinions. As we would expect, a fascinating picture emerged of what people appreciated or missed. There was, however, one overall theme which gradually emerged – the conviction of many that the top priority for the future growth of the Church was holiness.

Now holiness has had a bad press in recent years. It has not been given the attention which it used to receive, especially among evangelical Christians in the Keswick tradition.[1] That tradition, at its best, emphasised the inner power of the Holy Spirit to bring Christians gradually into Christlikeness. When the tradition was not freshly in touch with the living God or when the teaching came across second-hand, holiness was presented far more in terms of a series of dos and don'ts than the inner transformation brought about by the Holy Spirit.

One of the unstated reasons for the emergence of the charismatic renewal in the 1960s, especially among evangelical Christians, was disillusionment with what appeared to be a negative approach to personal holiness.

So many attractive facets of being alive in God's world were treated as devilish, dangerous or at least doubtful. A charismatic experience brought to many Christians a new freedom from the shibboleths of previous generations. Many previously no-go areas became acceptable, even priority, for these seeking to be disciples relevant to the contemporary world – for example, the arts, politics and socialising.

THE OPPOSITE POLE

As often happens, however, this development tended to be in reaction to previous negativity, rather than a straight-forward response to the call of God – with the inevitable result that a new extremism emerged at the opposite pole, in which the fall into rank disobedience of God's word was often sudden and blatant. Drunkenness, sexual immorality, financial dishonesty and unrestrained materialism are nothing new in the Church; neither is there necessarily any particularly Christian virtue in avoiding the deed while harbouring the thought. Nevertheless, one of the results of the previous generation's insistence on a particular expression of holiness was to increase the length and lessen the steepness of the downhill slope into practical unholiness.

Because fewer holds are thus barred, actual transgression of God's commandments is both more common and more popularly excusable, as anyone in pastoral ministry can readily testify. Now there is no place in the Christian Church for any condemnatory or recriminatory attitude. We are all equally sinners and the pound-of-flesh mentality comes from the Pharisees, not from the Saviour of the world. The story of the woman caught in adultery makes that plain (John 8: 1-11).

Jesus did, however, on that occasion tell the woman: 'go, and do not sin again.' It seems to me that there is a need once more to reaffirm the biblical call to personal holiness across the board, not in an attempt to rescue a compromising Church from the wicked world, but because it is precisely in such striking distinctiveness that the world will see the glory of the Lord. It is also worth recalling that, at the time Paul was writing this second letter to the Corinthians, the church at Corinth was still suffering from a fairly lax approach to personal holiness.

There had, in fact, been a significant slackening in the Corinthian slide into unholiness. In the first letter Paul had written pungently about their not merely tolerance, but arrogant pride, about unholiness in the Christian community – an unholiness that had seeped from the city into most parts of their life together. Some of these trends had been arrested, if not eliminated. Certain practices had been halted, but there was still a tendency to treat the call to holiness with less than total urgency.

So Paul feels bound to return to the theme of holiness with a few deft, but direct, strokes in 2 Corinthians 6: 14 to 7: 1. The teaching is straightforward, if not elementary, presumably because that is where Paul reckoned the Corinthians were. In today's *laissez-faire* attitude to holiness, we probably are at the same place and need the same direct and basic teaching.

AN UNEQUAL YOKE

Paul starts with a blunt directive: 'Do not be mismated with unbelievers.' This 'unequal yoke' was one of the most powerful phrases of my early Christian upbringing. I was left under no illusions that it was completely wrong for a Christian to get involved with, let alone marry, a non-Christian. I remember one teacher, expounding this passage, adding the comment that the same verse prohibited any business partnership between a Christian and a non-Christian.

Is Paul writing about marriage and business partnerships? Denney comments:

> The common application of this text to the marriage of Christians and non-Christians is legitimate, but too narrow. The text prohibits every kind of union in which the separate characters and interest of the Christian lose anything of their distinctiveness and integrity . . . we are to have no compromising connection with anything in the world which is alien to God . . . There always will be things and people to whom the Christian has to say 'No'.[2]

The wider and, at the same time, more probing application which Denney advocates is very appropriate in all kinds of contemporary situations. While reminding ourselves that the last thing Paul favoured was disengagement from costly, compassionate friendship with non-Christians,[3] we cannot evade the thrust of Paul's injunction not to become so intertwined with unbelievers that we compromise our distinctiveness. This tension – being fully involved but remaining clearly different – has always been of the essence of relevant discipleship, and there is no simple solution. Certainly the tension will never be resolved or removed this side of eternity, but 'we are the temple of the living God' (6: 16) and are therefore under an obligation to consider first the call to be different, not the desire to conform.

This call to be different will move us out of situations far less frequently than we think. Again, any tendency to avoid suffering will threaten to dislodge us from circumstances where God wants us to hold firm. The very fact of our being different will produce opposition and suffering. Paul seems to enjoin upon Christians, not disinvolvement, but non-identification. In many situations, this will mean remaining where we are, but very likely as thorns in the sides of our companions. That in itself will probably entail loss of promotion or preferment.

Paul's rhetorical questions in 6: 14 and 15 provide an acid test of our commitment to live distinctively as Christians. We are commissioned to live in the world as people committed to righteousness, called to be living ambassadors for Christ, men and women who operate by faith in God and who are conscious of being set apart as the distinctive dwelling-place of the Holy Spirit. These entirely positive statements provide a constructive framework for evaluating our personal holiness in a hostile world.

WHEN THE CHIPS ARE DOWN

And the world *is* hostile. Paul's personal perspective is provided in the opposites he describes in these same verses – iniquity, darkness, Satan, unbelief and idols. As with the positive phrases used to describe the identity-marks of the Christian, these words do not concentrate on outward details, but on underlying realities, the realities of a world organised without reference to God. Paul does not mean that everything the world does and offers is iniquity and idolatry. He is pointing out the incontrovertible truth that, when the chips are down, the unbelieving world is governed by priorities totally opposite to the priorities of the Christian.

Realistically, the Christian will usually be unable to discern whether it is right to press on in a situation until the chips *are* down. At that crisis the right answer might well be, 'No, I cannot go any further.' With the sensitive support and prayer of other Christians such a decision becomes an opportunity to grow in holiness, whether by choosing to stay in the situation or to come out. The criterion for making such a choice will surely not be the inherent difficulties and tension of the situation, but whether or not continuing in it will involve transgression of God's commandments – and the ten commandments still provide a searching and reliable guideline.

At this stage we need to look specifically at the application of Paul's teaching to marriage. It cannot be denied, except with rare speciousness, that his instruction in verse 14 includes a prohibition to Christians against marrying non-Christians (whatever else it may mean). If marriage means two becoming one, there is no way in which one person whose body is a temple of the Holy Spirit can, with integrity before God, justify being joined to someone whose body and being is not submitted to the Holy Spirit. In such an unequal partnership the chips are down before the partnership is contracted. The Christian has voluntarily submitted to the overall control of Jesus Christ as Lord; the non-Christian has not. The Christian, therefore, intends to refer every decision to a higher authority; the non-Christian does not.

In marriage there are countless situations, large and small, where the issue of who calls the shots is uppermost. It is self-deluding to think that these situations can be resolved by loving sensitivity, realistic commonsense, normal give and take, or some other way of behaving in a grown-up fashion. It simply does not work.

RHETORICAL QUESTIONS

Paul actually uses five phrases in his rhetorical questions in verses 14 and 15 which indicate the convictions he held about the nature of a truly equal marriage, where both husband and wife are pulling in the same direction in submission to the yoke of Christ. 'Partnership' has the connotation of sharing. It is God's intention that a man and a woman should share everything in Christian marriage. If one shares in Christ and the other does not, there is no true sharing in the very heart of the marriage – in worship, in prayer, in learning and growing together as Christians.

The second word, 'fellowship', covers all the experiences we have in common – experiences of God's love in special ways, of friendship with other Christians, of answered prayer, of the power of the Spirit, of the reality of forgiveness, of God's guidance through difficult times, of finding God's plan for our lives and walking in paths which he has already mapped out for us, of finding God's provision for our needs. Of course, there are many other experiences which a Christian and a non-Christian can share, which can contribute to a valuable and enjoyable friendship. But none of these is the same as two people being made one in Christ.

Paul next uses the Greek word from which we get 'symphony'. A Christian and a non-Christian have an inherent discord which, however mutual and sotto voce it may be at the beginning, will become increasingly strident. This lack of harmony becomes exposed in the bringing-up of children. I suppose it can only be a certain kind of Englishman who can honestly believe that being brought up as a Christian means nothing more than a good, decent education with a reasonable (always a reasonable) amount of religion thrown in. Anywhere else in the world, it is painfully recognised that only the home in which Jesus Christ is known and loved as Lord can provide a truly Christian upbringing – and that two converted parents are needed for such a demanding calling.

The last two words Paul uses emphasise, first, the common inheritance and, second, the stable foundation which God has provided for a Christian marriage. He intends a Christian couple to enter into all the fullness of what he has planned for their union. In general, this means that he wants every Christian marriage to be a visual aid to the world of what the spiritual union between Christ and his Church involves. As people look at the way husband and wife relate to each other in Christ, they will catch substantial glimpses of what is possible when God by his Spirit is united with an individual through Christ.

To explore the depths of such a calling is one of the unimaginable joys of Christian marriage. It is high tragedy for God to watch one of his children experiencing a union in which such a calling can never be pursued.

THE ONLY FOUNDATION

Equally, God has so arranged the ingredients of Christian marriage that in his Son Jesus there is a firm foundation on which a couple can build their partnership in face of all the storms which break so remorselessly on all marriages. If Jesus has not been made the foundation of both partners' lives, that stability is inevitably missing – one partner stands on rock, the other on sand.

The harsh realities of building a home and a marriage partnership were powerfully impressed on Rosemary and myself recently. Before we left Oxford, we invited about a dozen couples to our home for a meal and to discuss their experiences of married life and to pray together. I had had the privilege, in the previous two years, of taking or speaking at the weddings of each couple. From the outset of the general discussion a remarkable frankness prevailed. Some of the difficulties experienced by these couples were frightening in their intensity. In one case their honeymoon cottage in Ireland had been infested by poltergeists. In another case, the couple had faced a year's extremely painful readjustment after many years of living very independent lives as singles. The husband's job had also proved painfully disastrous, and a honeymoon baby had caused a very difficult pregnancy.

These couples were committed Christians, with their feet firmly on the stable foundation which is provided by God when Jesus Christ is Lord of a partnership. I shudder to think what might have happened if this foundation had not been in place for each partner.

As a pastor, I think I am aware of and sensitive to the

extreme difficulties facing committed Christian women, if they take seriously the words of Paul (which are consistent with overall biblical teaching) on the matter of marrying non-Christians. The statistics are all against them: in congregations in the Western world, the number of women exceeds the number of men in something like a two-to-one ratio. You only have to look around your own church next Sunday to check this out. If a Christian woman wants to be married, the pressure to make a wrong choice is extremely powerful.

It does, however, come down to a question of personal holiness – i.e. whether Christians are prepared to be distinctive in a world which plausibly glosses over the realism, let alone the rightness, of listening to God's word.

A COSTLY PRIORITY

Holiness is a costly priority at every level for each Christian – so costly that we can easily despair. What is the way forward? 'Since we have these promises, beloved' (2 Cor. 7: 1). In the last three verses of chapter 6 Paul quotes several such promises from the Old Testament, taken from Ezekiel, Jeremiah, Isaiah and Hosea (Ezek. 37: 27; Jer. 31: 1; Isa. 52: 1; Hos. 1: 10; Isa. 43: 6). God has committed himself to his people – 'I will live in them and move among them... I will be their God... I will welcome you... I will be a father to you.' These are the sure promises of a God who never changes. Personal holiness is the result of closing with these promises, taking them as promises for our daily lives, and seeing God go to work to make them come true.

All these uncompromising promises God has sealed with the blood of his Son. In his death Jesus fulfilled and guaranteed every promise of God. As Paul declared towards the beginning of this letter, Jesus is the Yes and the Amen to all the promises of God (2 Cor. 1: 20). Peter called these promises 'precious and very great', and was bold enough to assert that 'through these you may escape from the corruption which is in the world because of passion, and become partakers of the divine nature' (2 Pet. 1: 4).

There is, then, both a negative and a positive side to personal holiness. Peter's particular emphasis underlines the need decisively to reject anything which smells of 'corruption' or unrighteousness. That decisive rejection creates the atmosphere in which we can respond more eagerly to God's call to become like his Son, Jesus. As Paul puts it, 'let us cleanse ourselves from every defilement of body and spirit, and make holiness perfect in the fear of God' (2 Cor. 7: 1).

In essence, therefore, there is no alternative for the Christian who takes the lordship of Jesus seriously. We are to apply ourselves wholeheartedly to working out the holiness which God has given us in Jesus: he *is* our righteousness and our sanctification.[4] The advice I was frequently given in my early years as a Christian is still as relevant as ever: 'Would Jesus do that?'

10

SPACE IN RELATIONSHIPS

In chapter three we looked at the subject of pastoral care. In this chapter we take a further look at the same theme, but in the wider context of relationships in general. 'Give me room' is a common cry in today's world, especially when someone feels hemmed in by those around him. A kind of interpersonal claustrophobia has begun to afflict many Christians, especially after they have experienced oppressive closeness in relationships in a given church-fellowship.

Several factors have produced this lack of elbow-room in many congregations. Sometimes it is simply a matter of smallness: everybody knows everyone else very well and privacy is hard to come by. A certain kind of church is also extremely demanding on the time and energies of its members, soaking up more and more spare hours in its in-group activities. Such an incessant round of church activities hems many Christians into a very limited sphere of social contacts, effectively cutting them off from wider and more rounded relationships.

OPPRESSIVE INTENSITY

One of the more powerful influences is rather more subtle

and stems from the very seriousness with which certain Christians take their faith and discipleship. This seriousness can easily slip into an oppressive intensity. The general atmosphere is one of wholeheartedness – which cannot be bad in itself – but it can easily degenerate into not just personal seriousness, but over-zealous involvement in other people's lives. The word used in my younger days was 'keenness' – if someone was really 'keen', it meant he took his faith seriously, and took everybody else's faith (or lack of it) seriously.

It is fairly clear that the dividing-line between wholehearted discipleship and oppressive intensity is rather thin. Different people will draw it in different places. In the days of George Whitefield, the Wesleys and the Evangelical Revival, more traditional Englishmen found the 'enthusiasm' of such Christians extremely distasteful. I think we need to be careful in identifying the tendency which worries me today and, I know, many other Christians. I mean the way well-meaning people crowd their fellow-believers, giving them little or no room to be themselves, to get on with their own lives, to tackle their own problems and challenges, and to develop their relationship with God in their own way. I think more clues to this syndrome will emerge as we take a closer look at Paul's *cri de coeur* in chapters 6 and 7 of 2 Corinthians (6: 11–13; 7: 2–4).

A literal translation of 6: 12 would run: 'We have not shut you up, Corinthians, in a narrow place in our relationship with you; but you have shut yourselves up in a narrow place as far as your gut-level feelings are concerned.' The word used twice in this verse is exactly the same as the one Paul used earlier in the chapter when talking about the inevitably 'narrow places' (translated 'calamities' in the RSV) in which he found himself as a Christian minister. However unavoidable we shall find narrowness in our circumstances, it is not necessary inwardly in our emotions or in our relationships with others.

The Corinthians had shut themselves up emotionally as far as Paul was concerned. He could not get through to them, he could not get inside them to find out how they were really ticking. It was not, apparently, due to any reluctance to be open on Paul's side: 'Our mouth is open to you, Corinthians; our heart is wide.' Paul, at any rate, had found space to be himself in his relationships with the Corinthians. Indeed, the evidence of the Acts of the Apostles and of his letters in the rest of the New Testament reveals a warm-blooded, spontaneous, straightforward man.

NOT SIMPLY TEMPERAMENTAL

But it would be a mistake to see Paul's openness and internal freedom as a temperamental phenomenon. He makes it plain himself that he has been taught by the Holy Spirit how to relate in Christ to others. There are two cryptic, but highly suggestive, clues in this passage, contained in the following phrases: 'I speak as to children' (6: 13), and 'You are in our hearts, to die together and to live together' (7: 3).

In talking to the Corinthians 'as to children', Paul is pleading with them to drop their inner complexity and their chary aloofness from him, and to trust him. Children are far more truthful than adults and they will usually relate spontaneously to those whom they meet, not least towards God. Jesus made it plain that childlikeness is of the essence of the kingdom of God, and in few contexts is such childlikeness more fundamental than in the way we relate to one another. Paul had learned, under the instruction of the Holy Spirit, to be childlike with the Corinthians, to be open, generous and trusting. He longed for them to respond in kind.

The other suggestive phrase is equally full of theological truth. Paul does not use words lazily or haphazardly: when he uses the phrase, 'to die together and to live together', he uses the words carefully in both their sequence and in their significance.[1] We have seen already that, in the kingdom of God, death always precedes life.[2] So, when Paul uses the phrases in this way, he is referring to the daily experience of dying-and-living with Jesus as it applies to his own relationship with the Christians at Corinth. 'You are in our hearts, to die together and to live together' – in other words, Paul had room within his heart for the Corinthians and there to cope with the painful tension of being in Christ together without hemming them in or crowding them: they had room to be themselves in Christ.

So Paul was completely committed to encouraging the Corinthians to grow as Christians, but he did not intend ever to envelop them in a stifling way with his concern. It was entirely up to them to respond to the promptings of the Spirit. So far, they had failed to open up to Paul in the way he had been open with them. But Paul steadfastly resisted the temptation to force them to be open: there was space in his relationship with them.

CROWDING ONE ANOTHER

A number of questions inevitably raise themselves in our minds at this point, centring mainly on what attitudes and behaviour tend to crowd people and how we can create more space for and with one another. Paul's comments in this passage, which is almost an aside to his main argument, are very illuminating. Certain things, he says, must *not* happen if there is going to be space in relationships.

First, 'we have wronged no one' (7: 2). This is referring to any unjust action in our relationships, in which we transgress God's laws and thereby cause definite harm to another person by our behaviour. I can think of several situations over the years where a Christian has resorted to completely unscrupulous actions to establish or maintain control over another Christian's life – perhaps through breaking confidences by talking about the person to a third party, or through deliberately creating mistrust towards the other person by sowing doubts about his/her reliability or integrity. There is also a pernicious tendency to use shared confidences virtually as fuel for blackmail: 'If you don't do what I say, I shall have to go and tell the vicar.'

Second, 'we have corrupted no one' (7: 2). This word 'may refer to money, morals or doctrine'[3] – any way in which a Christian, normally an older and respected member of a church, can abuse a position of trust with someone who has come to them for guidance or help. It is sadly true that such situations are often allowed to degenerate to the level where a young Christian is corrupted. Such corruption can take place without any overtly immoral behaviour. For example, it is all too easy to play around with a person's emotions, especially where a sexual attraction has been aroused: it could be either heterosexual or homosexual. Another example of such corruption is the way certain people deliberately set about undermining the 'simple faith' of those who have recently been converted, either by dismissing the reality of their experience or by systematically sowing doubt. This happens a lot in university circles, where new believers are bound to come across scepticism in high ecclesiastical places.

Third, Paul maintains that 'we have taken advantage of no one' (7: 2). This word is used consistently in the New Testament to describe covetousness or greed. In the present context it refers to using people, wanting more and more from them in our relationship with them. It is essentially a 'me-centred' attitude to relationships. We keep them going because they help *us* and because, perhaps, we *need* the relationships. It is evident that such an attitude is, by definition, not creating space for the other person, because there is no dying to self-interest and therefore no experience of the new life of Jesus to share.

SEARCHING STRICTURES

I find these three strictures of Paul extremely searching. If I harm, corrupt or use another person, I have shut them up in a very narrow place – and it is extremely difficult to prise such a prisoner free to relate to others once more. There is deep trauma involved for such a person in facing the possibility of being locked up in an even smaller cell. Many Christians are closed to others today, because somewhere along the line they started to be open and were badly hurt.

Paul's positive statements about his relationship with the Corinthians are equally instructive. First, he says, 'I have great confidence in you' (7: 4). He has already used the word in this letter in describing the boldness[4] which characterises all those into whose hearts God has shone by his Spirit – boldness before God and boldness before men, totally unlike Moses who needed to cover up. So here Paul testifies to the boldness he feels in the presence of the Corinthians, boldness to be himself. He does not need to pretend: when he feels let down, hurt or angry, he is free to let them know how he feels. When someone has this amount of inner room to move in his personal relation-ships, he is free to be himself. When we are inhibited or tentative with others, it shows a lack of space – for us and for them.

GENUINE PRIDE

Paul continues by affirming the 'great pride' he has in the Corinthians. He loves to talk about them to others, because he is genuinely proud of them. This is akin to two people in love, who want to tell the world and are not ashamed to have everyone know – and, indeed, be present. Many relationships within the Church exist in secrecy, because the people concerned know that there is little or nothing to be proud of. Whatever such folk may fondly believe, there is no space in a relationship which cannot face exposure to the light. Any element of secrecy spells danger and bondage.

Third, Paul says of his relationship with the Corinthians that he is 'filled with comfort' (7: 4). He means that, in spite of all its problems, the relationship is one that basically brings him encouragement and strength, not turmoil. The word Paul uses is the same word used for the Holy Spirit, the Comforter. A relationship governed by the Holy Spirit will produce the same results as the Holy Spirit produces in a believer – love, joy, peace, long-suffering, gentleness, faithfulness, meekness, self-control. These are the qualities in any relationship with true space in it.

JOY IN AFFLICTION

Lastly, Paul can honestly say of his relationship with the Corinthians, 'I am overjoyed' (7: 4), even though he was in the middle of 'great affliction' or pressure, some of which was linked to the Corinthians. The joy did not remove the pressures, it permeated them. So Paul was no idealist in describing this relationship. He never expected it to be all warmth and light, but he could look at it realistically and still come up with the verdict: my relationship with the Corinthians is characterised by openness, brings me great pride, is a source of real comfort, and fills me with joy.

At this point we need to remind ourselves that Paul was an apostle, vested with unique authority of a kind which is available to no Christian minister of any kind today. Yet he never at any stage attempted to play God with the Corinthians. He strove to give them the space to be themselves which he himself had come to appreciate. He did not see his authority as a licence to dictate or to bully, to stifle or to constrict. In fact, he explicitly states later: 'our authority, which the Lord gave for building you up and not for destroying you' (2 Cor. 10: 8).

It is of the utmost importance, therefore, that all Christians entrusted with visible or accepted authority over others ask the question: 'Am I in any sense playing God to anyone, either in counselling or in teaching or simply by my strength of personality?' We also ought to put ourselves in the shoes of those whom we are in danger of locking up in a narrow place by our behaviour or attitude. It is central to what God has done for us in Jesus that he has won for us space in our relationships. We are free to be ourselves with God and with others – are we allowing others the same freedom, the same room to be themselves?

11

REPENTANCE

When a Christian in a local church steps out of line by breaking one of God's commandments, fellow-believers are deeply hurt in many painful ways. When we talk of repentance, therefore, it is important to understand that invariably this is a matter for the body of believers, not just for one or two individuals. This was certainly the case at Corinth. We do not know the details, but Paul had clearly been personally pained to discover the lax way in which the Corinthians had approached a particularly unacceptable case of sin in the church fellowship. They had not dealt with the offender in an effective or proper manner. Paul had been compelled to write a very strong letter to them, which had not received any answer. While in Macedonia, about 300 miles north of Corinth, Paul had sent Titus to find out what had happened.

In briefing Titus, Paul had shared with him both his concern for the situation at Corinth and his basic confidence in the people there.[1] Things had been extremely serious, but Paul retained his expectations that the Corinthians knew how to take a rebuke and how to cope with flagrant sin in their midst. In Paul's understanding of the gospel and its practical implications for life in the local church, what was desperately needed was repentance – unadorned, full-blooded, God-directed repentance, not just feeling sorry or saying sorry, but a fundamental change of attitude, accompanied by specific action to prove the genuineness of the repentance.

SHALLOW REMORSE

In this passage (2 Cor. 7: 5–16) Paul covers the theme of repentance with considerable thoroughness, not so much by explicit statements as by his own commentary on how the Corinthians reacted to the contents of his stern letter and the visit of Titus. Today repentance is often a shallow and introverted matter, sharing little of the ingredients of the Corinthian experience. As Christians we often fail to express proper repentance for the ways in which we walk all over other people in sitting very lightly to God's will. When we do start to taste the fruit of our un-Christlike behaviour, the repentance we then feel can often be characterised more by remorse for the problems we have brought upon ourselves, than by genuine penitence for the way we have defied God and trampled on his love – quite apart from any damage done to other people.

There are probably many reasons for this shallowness: for example, we have noted earlier[2] the anaemic interpretation often given to the death of Christ, particularly the reality of God's righteous anger towards sin. Perhaps the most pervasive cause, however, lies in our own self-centredness. We find it very difficult to distance ourselves from the misery and difficulty which our selfish disobedience inevitably brings upon us. The result is that we rarely can place ourselves in the shoes of those whom we have damaged or hurt; still less can we accurately sense the grief and anger which as our Father and Saviour, God himself feels when we turn our backs on him.

True repentance is a very painful and costly experience. It involves personal suffering, but it leads to greater glory being given to God and more glory being written into our inner beings. It is always difficult simply to climb down and say sorry, even in the most normal situations with the people we love most. I frequently find I have to swallow my pride and apologise to my wife and – increasingly as they are in or around the teenage years – to my four children. There is probably no habit more eloquent of Christian destinctiveness than proper repentance: the world does not believe in it; those who wield power and influence rarely apologise or admit personal responsiblity – when they do, it is usually after great delay, much persuasion, personal justification, and with at least one finger pointing away from themselves. That is human nature.

Paul gives a superb summary of the options in verse 10: 'godly grief produces a repentance that leads to salvation and brings no regret, but worldly grief produces death.' There is a lot of breast-beating and lamenting in the world at large. There is no shortage of tears or of sorrow. But it gets people nowhere; it simply accentuates the 'death' already present through human sinfulness, frailty and selfishness. Nobody is released or cleansed by this kind of sorrow. Time may eventually bring more ability to cope, and those of a stronger constitution or more self-sufficient temperament may be able to make something positive out of the future. But the air has never been cleared and wounds have not been healed: this much has been made very plain in many cases where personal prayer and counselling have been needed.

THE ROAD TO BE TRAVELLED

There is another way, the way which Paul describes as 'the pain which is according to God' (literal translation of the phrase rendered 'godly grief'). The phrase suggests a road which must be travelled, not a feeling which comes upon us. It also is clear that there is a destination we reach on this painful road, beyond which we can expect to be able to look back without any regrets. That destination is the point where we enter more fully into the salvation of the Lord than we ever have done before – the action or attitude which required repentance has been turned, by the grace of God, into an opportunity to know in a fresh way his forgiveness and also the freedom to be different.

It is entirely unrealistic to suggest that we can always expect to forget such extremely painful experiences in our Christian pilgrimage, especially when we have been on the receiving end. Some Christians indicate that God actually blots out the very memory of what has happened, once there has been repentance leading to an experience of his forgiveness: 'we can forgive *and* forget,' they say, 'because God forgives *and* forgets.' From personal experience I can vouch for the fact that, in time, we *do* forget the details of certain experiences in the past. Far more importantly, we find we can, by the grace of God, look back at traumatic events with equanimity and without rancour – but only when genuine repentance according to God's way has properly cleared the air and allowed a clean start.

What is involved in such repentance becomes more apparent as we look more closely at Paul's comments on the Corinthian experience. The Revised Standard Version obscures the issues by its epithet 'godly', used three times in successive verses (9, 10 and 11) to render the phrase we earlier translated 'according to God', or following God's way. Denney comments:

> The sorrow according to God is that in which the sinner is conscious of his sin in relation to the Holy One, and feels that its inmost soul of pain and guilt is this, that he has fallen away from the grace and friendship of God ... Anything else – the sorrow, for example, which is bounded by the selfish interests of the sinner, and is not due to his sinful act, but only to its painful consequences – is the sorrow of the world.[3]

SIN AGAINST GOD

All sin is, first and foremost, sin against God. However important it is to stress that no man is an island and that we can never sin purely privately (someone is always affected by even the most solitary transgression of God's commandments), we must above all be clear about the way God himself is personally involved as Father in the sins of his children. As a father of four I am inevitably and deeply affected by the behaviour of my children. I am most profoundly affected in my relationship with them, not so much by any less relational factor such as the family reputation or the impact on their own character of the way they behave. Those things *do* bother me, but above all else I want to keep my friendship with them in the open. When they go against my will, that friendship is damaged.

True repentance, therefore, is produced by a sorrow which is directed towards God when we have gone against his will. When this sorrow is present, it will lead to appropriate action in connection with those affected by our behaviour – as it did with the Corinthians in their relationship with Paul. By apparently flouting the will of God in not facing up to the offender in their midst, they had caused Paul immense pain. He had written to them with directness, not because he primarily had in mind 'the one who did the wrong nor on account of the one who suffered the wrong', but because it was of great importance to establish their relationship once again 'in the sight of God' (2 Cor. 7: 12). The two involved in the actual offence did receive the required ministry, but Paul's stress on the relationship between himself and the Corinthians underlines the way a personal breakdown between two individuals can have very widespread repercussions.

A RISKY MANOEUVRE

Paul, we should notice, had to go out on a limb to bring

about the proper repentance of the Corinthians. He had to risk complete – and perhaps permanent – alienation. There is always such a risk in such a course of action, but the risks involved in non-confrontation are far greater: acceptance of sin in the fellowship with the inevitable spiritual death which that brings. I know that there have been occasions in my own ministry when I have shrunk from the direct confrontation necessary for true repentance. The result has always been a steady deterioration in the situation; the air has never been cleared, and there has been a residue of spiritual death.

Even though Paul was ready to take the risky course of confronting the Corinthians by his blunt approach, there was one thing he apparently never did. He did not speak disparagingly of the Corinthians to other people, even to Titus when he commissioned him to be his messenger. In telling Titus of what had been going on in Corinth, he expressed pride and confidence in the church members, not bitterness or criticism. As Denney remarks:

> What in most cases of estrangement makes reconciliation hard is that the estranged have allowed themselves to speak of each other to outsiders in a way that cannot be forgotten or got over. But even when the tension between Paul and the Corinthians was at its height, he boasted of them to Titus ... He could say severe things to them, but he would never disparage or malign them to other people.[4]

This tendency to go to third parties instead of going, where at all possible, directly to the other person is one of the most destructive habits in the local church. Gossip is often rationalised into respectability by those who, however painfully they have been treated, are under divine obligation to go *first* to the person who has caused the pain.[5]

Some final insights on what goes to make up true

repentance are provided by Paul's grateful exclamation in
2 Corinthians 7: 11: 'For see what earnestness this godly
grief has produced in you, what eagerness to clear
yourselves, what indignation, what alarm, what longing,
what zeal, what punishment!' Earlier, Titus had testified
to their longing, mourning and zeal for Paul (2 Cor. 7: 7).
This series of evocative words give some indication of
what Paul understands by repentance.

GENUINE SORROW

The issue at stake was, we remind ourselves, the
relationship between Paul and the Corinthians. Through
their highhandedness the Corinthians had imperilled it. It
needed to be put back on the right footing. Paul had taken
the costly, painful and risky initiative. The situation
required proper repentance on the part of the Corinthians.
They had to demonstrate genuine sorrow for what they
had done to Paul, and then give solid proof of their
commitment to Paul in future. The words Paul uses, in
such a context, are very illuminating. The following
paraphrase gives a good sense of the words:

> See what earnestness it worked out in you, how keen you
> were to clear yourselves from just reproach, how
> indignant with the chief offender, how alarmed as to
> what the consequences might be, how eager for my
> forgiveness and return, how zealous in condemning
> evil, how stern in punishing it.[6]

In fact, the Corinthians treated the situation with full
seriousness. They did not bring forward extenuating
circumstances. They did not draw favourable comparisons with the way other churches dealt with the
apostle. They did not point the finger elsewhere. They did
not minimise the importance of the sinful behaviour of

their member (whatever they might have done in the early stages of the crisis). They did not close their eyes to the facts and hope the trouble would go away. They did not underplay the value and significance of their relationship with Paul or begin to treat it as dispensable. They did not flinch from the pain of administering firm discipline to the offender.

All these factors stress the 'godly grief' of the Corinthians. They show that God's attitude and God's interests had become uppermost in the Corinthians' approach to their broken relationship with Paul. They were now determined to ensure that Paul's mind was at rest and that the future would not bring any repetition of the breakdown. This is borne out in a similar paraphrase of the way Titus reported back to Paul: 'He gave a most welcome report of how you longed for reconciliation with me, how you lamented the trouble you had caused, how eagerly you espoused my cause.'[7]

This passage, therefore, gives us a model of how to go about the painful and difficult process of mending a broken relationship within the family of God. It shows that repentance towards God is the essential springboard for reconciliation. God has laid down the route we must travel: both the parties involved have specific responsibilities in the matter. If we were prepared to travel this route, many bruised Christians in churches everywhere would find healing and hope.

12

GENEROSITY

As I sit down to write this chapter, we as a family have just returned from a harvest festival service in a small village church in north Cornwall. The church was beautifully decorated with symbols of the huge bounty which the glorious summer of 1984 has provided. Apparently, farmers are saying that this has been probably the richest harvest in living memory, and the previous two years were almost record years as well. In his sermon today the vicar quite rightly stressed the obligation of those blessed in such a signal way to find ways of sharing the good things of God's creation with those less fortunate. He applied it locally and internationally.

I do not think I was alone in sensing in the atmosphere a fairly stiff resistance to the vicar's remarks. Whenever money is raised in a church gathering, there is usually an aura of embarrassment mixed with resentment – embarrassment on the part of those who have to talk about it, resentment in the hearts of those who think the way they acquire and spend their money is a private matter.

AN IMPRESSIVE TRACK RECORD

Evangelical Christians have an extremely good record,

compared with other Christians, in the matter of giving –
just ask the treasurers of Anglican dioceses in England or
look at the diocesan accounts, if you want to see the
evidence. Most dioceses would be even more precarious
economically, were it not for the amount given by
evangelical parishes.

One of the significant results of any true movement of
the Spirit in a congregation is always increased giving.
The more open to God and to one another Christians
become, the more straightforward will be their approach
to any discussion of money.

When, however, we look closely at Paul's discussion of
money in chapters 8 and 9 of 2 Corinthians, we cannot
help thinking that he had found a freedom with the
Christians at Corinth which is all too rare today. He also
makes it plain that money is absolutely central to
Christian discipleship. There is one particular phrase
which goes right to the heart of the matter: he emphasises
that the way the Corinthians respond with their cash will
demonstrate 'your loyalty to the gospel of Christ which
you profess' (9: 13 TEV). As we look at the details of Paul's
discussion, we shall probably find a radical challenge to
the way we think and behave in money matters.

I believe that, inherent to our commitment to Jesus as
Lord, there is an approach to our money which is far more
radical than, even at our most generous, we normally
envisage. Once again, it goes right against the grain of our
human nature, because it reaches its glorious fulfilment
only through considerable suffering. In this sense, it cuts
right across the prosperity teaching so popular today.
Such teaching encourages Christians to believe that God
wants his children to be wealthy, to enjoy the good things
of life, and to lack nothing they want. There is, inevitably,
a strong emphasis on giving: but Christians are urged to
give because it will bring back to them great material
blessing.

This stress is nothing more or less than a scarcely

disguised appeal to our inner selfishness and greed. We only have to look at the more blatant appeals to our covetousness made through television quiz programmes and millionaire promises in the daily newspapers, and we can appreciate how far the way of the world has penetrated the Church.

PAUL'S PRIORITY

Paul has a totally different approach to the theme of generous giving. As a matter of policy, he made a top priority of the business of collecting money for the poor Christians in Jerusalem. Wherever he travelled, he appealed strongly to churches to contribute to 'the relief of the saints' (8: 4). He regarded this relief fund to be as central to the gospel as evangelism, holiness, repentance or love. It was a matter of obedience, not an optional extra. He faced the Corinthians with their responsibilities with complete frankness, because of the 'perfect confidence' (7: 16) and openness he always practised towards them.

Nonetheless, however urgent and essential he regarded the subject of giving, he never lapsed into a legalistic imposition upon the Corinthians. There is, for example, no mention of tithing in this – the fullest single treatment of the subject in the Bible – discussion of giving. In fact, Paul's basis is manifestly nothing else but the inexhaustible grace of God: the passage begins and ends with explicit reference to God's grace and its impact on people's lives (8: 1; 9: 15).

Paul sees generous giving as a practical example of God's grace at work in a Christian's life. The same Greek word, *charis*, is used four times at the beginning of chapter eight: it is translated, on three occasions, 'this gracious work'. The heart of generous giving is explained in verse 9: 'You know the grace of our Lord Jesus Christ, that though he was rich, yet for your sake he became poor, so that by his poverty you might become rich.' Christlike generosity is prepared to give like that, to become poor so that others might become rich. Paul later modifies this revolutionary principle only slightly, when he introduces the principle of 'equality' as the practical guideline for our giving (8: 14).

He is clear that he does not mean that 'others should be eased and you burdened' (8: 14) in any permanent way. Nevertheless, he does expect that 'your abundance at the present time should supply their want' (8: 14). Paul envisages the time, presumably in the not-too-distant future, when 'their abundance will supply your want.' We can see, therefore, that he sees equality in terms of generously giving away what we have in abundance to meet the needs of those who have less than enough.

MUTUAL INTERDEPENDENCE

Paul passionately believed in mutual interdependence in the international family of God. Four times towards the end of chapter eight, he mentions the close fellowship in mission and ministry enjoyed by 'the churches' with which he has been connected (8: 18, 19, 23, 24). These churches were in constant communication with one another, in the very limited way such contact could be maintained in the first century as compared with the generation of the microchip. There is little or no excuse today for failing to keep informed about the needs of other Christians elsewhere. If we courageously and consistently applied Paul's principle of equality, we would surely be giving far more generously to God's Church overseas. The implications for our own life style are naturally considerable, but Paul seems not to be particularly interested in such factors. If one church enjoys abundance and another experiences want, there is only one way to go – the way Jesus went in becoming poor for us.

The example of rich generosity which Paul chooses to portray for the Corinthians is that of the Macedonian Christians (8: 1). Here were people in 'extreme poverty' (8: 2) – the phrase literally means 'down-to-the-depths beggarhood'. They could not have had a lower standard of living: they were on their beam ends. They had virtually nothing they could give, even if they wanted to. But because they *did* want to, they gave to the Jerusalem relief fund: 'For they gave according to their means... and beyond their means, of their own free will' (8: 3). They saw the opportunity to help Jewish Christians as 'a favour', a privilege. There was, in fact, nothing that the Christians of Philippi and Thessalonica would not joyfully hand over to the Lord, or to Paul as his representative.

Such generosity is astonishing; it is a miracle – possible only through the grace of God at work in human hearts unlocking them to behave like Jesus. There are countless examples today of such generosity in the midst of great suffering and abject poverty – I have seen it in Chile and in Uganda. Such Christians find their inspiration and example in Jesus. He suffered and he gave; he loved to the very limits of his resources, and even beyond them; he chose to lay down his life in his love for us; he made himself totally available to his Father as he freely handed himself over to death.

SCRUPULOUS CARE

Before we look at the further teaching Paul gives on the privilege of generous giving, it is worth simply noting the scrupulous care which he takes to ensure that the money is properly collected, carefully administered, and safely handed over to the right people. Spontaneity and joy in giving away money must always be channelled with this integrity. Paul was concerned that there should be no blame attached to him or anyone else (8: 20). To that end he was prepared to assign to this task only someone fully tried and tested for his honesty in financial affairs. Why such strict attention to detail? 'We aim at what is honourable not only in the Lord's sight but also in the sight of men' (8: 21). Sadly, this is not consistently done today. Christians are no more immune to temptations of this kind than anyone else.

In 9: 6-15, Paul explains the underlying considerations to be taken into account in Christian giving. He starts with a general truth with specific application to the matter in hand: 'Sow sparingly, reap sparingly ... sow bountifully, reap bountifully.' He is once again drawing a spiritual lesson about God's activity from the Creator's work in nature. Earlier, Paul had shown how death precedes life in the kingdom of God, as in Nature. Here he makes the self-evident point that you cannot get a rich harvest from meagre sowing.

It is misleading to suggest that Paul is here recommending generous giving away of our money on the grounds that we shall get a lot of money in return. He is stating a law of nature and applying it to the Christian life: God is the author of both, and is no man's debtor. It is his own nature to give and, in giving, he receives. When we act like him, we find that we receive in many different ways – 'you will be enriched in every way for great generosity' (9: 11). All that Paul does promise in material terms is 'enough' – not enough to satisfy our desire for more than we need, but enough to go on giving, to 'provide in abundance for every good work' (9: 8).

A GIVE-AWAY ATTITUDE

Paul, surely, is advocating a give-away attitude to our money and our possessions, not clinging on to them either by selfish hoarding or in secure investment or for self-indulgence. At this very moment a film on television is showing some Christians in Zaire meeting an English traveller in the heart of Africa. They are making a present to this stranger, Michael Wood, of some chickens. He comments: 'The poor have given me more than they can afford.' The joy on those African faces is the perfect commentary on Paul's teaching. Jesus urged us in similar vein: 'give, and it will be given you; good measure, pressed down, shaken together, running over, will be put into your lap. For the measure you give will be the measure you get back' (Luke 6: 38).

The joy of these African Christians – and they are not exceptional on that amazing continent – provides an example of Paul's statement, 'God loves a cheerful giver' (2 Cor. 9: 9) – the Greek word gives us our English word 'hilarious'. The love of God shone out of the faces of Michael Wood's new-found friends; his love for the traveller and his love for the Africans were equally manifest. When this love has grasped our hearts, there will be little room left for the reluctance which so easily marks our giving. As someone is reported to have said once in a church service: 'Hallelujah! Here comes the collection!'

In his uninhibited concentration on spontaneity, joy, hilarity and generosity, Paul does not neglect the need for planned and thoughtful giving. He does not want the Corinthians to be haphazard: 'Each one must do as he has made up his mind' (9: 7). The unlimited grace of God calls for a sober decision on the part of each Christian: overwhelming gratitude and careful decision-making need to come together, but the carefulness is to be a carefulness to glorify God.

There is no shortage of promises about what God will do if we act generously in this way. The verbs alone in verses 8–10 are eloquent: 'God will provide ... supply ... multiply ... increase.' He is committed to giving in abundance. We shall, therefore, discover in sacrificial giving the release of the Holy Spirit in every direction: 'and increase the harvest of your righteousness' (9: 10).

What is more, God will be glorified by such obedience to the gospel.

If we remain under any doubt about the central place of such generosity in Christian discipleship, Paul removes it in the short cry of praise at the end of the chapter: 'Thanks be to God for his inexpressible gift!' (9: 15). God is the supreme giver. It is in his nature to give. He has given Jesus to us. He has given himself in Jesus. He has given us all things in Jesus. The man or the woman who lets Jesus be Lord will give with the same kind of generosity, so that others might become equally enriched. There is suffering in that; there is also glory.

13

THE DEVIL AND ALL HIS WORKS

From the way some Christians talk and behave, it is easy to get the impression that the real cause of anything unpleasant is the devil. His influence, indeed his presence, is readily seen everywhere. When this conviction is taken to excess, a very unhealthy atmosphere begins to pervade a local church, in which Satan is blamed for virtually everything, demons are regularly discerned and dealt with, and not much room is left for such realities as individual responsibility for behaviour or the complexity of human experience.

At its most naive and most dangerous, such over-emphasis on the devil betrays a fundamental dualism in people's thinking: the world is seen almost literally as two spheres – the one in which God rules and everything is light and truth, the other in which the devil holds sway and causes nothing but darkness, evil and misery. Such a world-view inevitably leads to several parodies of Christian truth. The most serious parody sees Jesus and Satan, not just as in opposition, but as two rival – and equivalent – contenders for the allegiance of human beings. Because these two masters are seen as equally able to hold our obedience, Christians are perceived as slipping from one sphere of sovereignty to the other like a Jekyll and Hyde.

This very depressing view of Christian experience has

signally failed to appreciate, let alone to accept, the inherent paradox of being a Christian, summed up in the 'now' and the 'not yet' of Pauline theology. Paul clearly teaches that we have been translated from the kingdom of darkness into the kingdom of God's Son.[1] He equally makes plain that we are involved in a cosmic conflict with the powers of darkness,[2] in which we are exposed to 'the wiles of the devil' and 'the flaming darts of the evil one'.

NOW AND NOT YET

The only consistent, though paradoxical, way to hold these two truths together is to recognise that in Christ we *now* live in the kingdom of God, but that we have *not* yet been fully extricated from the sphere of Satan's influence. Until God's kingdom is finally consummated, we remain vulnerable to the devil's power. We do not, however, slide from one sphere of sovereignty into the other and back again. On the contrary, precisely because we are children of God's kingdom we are targets of Satan's attacks. To be a Christian does not bring immunity from these; rather, it steps up the enemy action.

The corollary of this perspective is that God is at work in all that we experience as Christians, whatever the nature and originating cause. The triumph of Jesus over Satan through his death and resurrection certainly assures us of ultimate victory; but it also indicates that everything which Satan, as 'the god of this world' (2 Cor. 4: 4), activates in our daily lives is subject to the significance of Good Friday and Easter. As Christians we do not pass like yo-yos backwards and forwards between Jesus's sovereignty and Satan's sovereignty.

Because this situation is full of paradox and of the tension inherent in all paradox, there seems to be no simple way of defining precisely where and how Satan is operating, as distinct from several other influences which can affect our daily lives. The perspective of the New Testament as a whole encourages us to be alert to the variety, force and subtlety of the devil's activity – but not to give him too much credit or attention. We live on the other side of Easter and this fact should determine our daily living, not any preoccupation with Satanic activity.

Having made this point, I want to emphasise that Christian discipleship and ministry will always be characterised by spiritual conflict. At times this comes right out into the open in naked encounter with frighteningly blatant forces of darkness. These periods can be protracted, and certain Christians engaged on the front line often have little relief. For most Christians for most of the time, it is a question of pressing steadily on to establish complete possession of territory still plagued by sporadic guerrilla activity, but basically subjugated. Peace is not properly secured until hostilities of both kinds have ceased, and this will not happen until the return of Christ.

A STRIKING PROFILE

Against this background, Paul's own comments in 2 Corinthians about the activity of Satan take on fresh significance. Because this letter is uniquely concerned with the realities of Christian ministry, and because Paul describes in unvarnished terms the painful suffering involved in being an ambassador for Christ, the profile he gives to the devil is all the more striking. As we examine his description, we shall discover the balanced perspective he provides.

There are seven, direct or indirect, references to Satan in this letter – 2: 10–11; 4: 3, 4; 6: 15; 10: 3ff; 11: 2, 3; 11: 13–15; 12: 7. In the first passage Paul asserts: 'We are not ignorant of his designs.' This last word refers to the way Satan thinks: it is the same word used in 4: 4 ('minds'), 10: 5 ('thought') and 11: 3 ('thoughts'). Satan has a mind and uses it. Paul is able to claim knowledge of Satan's mind. He has obtained this partly from the explanation provided by the Old Testament Scriptures, partly from his own experience as a Christian disciple, but mainly from the complete exposure of Satan provoked by the ministry, sufferings, trial, death and resurrection of Jesus.

Jesus unmasked Satan. He challenged him in his own territory. Time and time again, especially in Mark's gospel, we read of Jesus uncovering the works of the devil by his authoritative presence and preaching. Hitherto, the devil had been able to keep the extent of his activity secret: darkness could thrive because the light had not been shining. By his steady obedience to his Father, Jesus forced the devil to play every card in his pack, even to the final desperate fling of getting rid of the Son of God in death. This 'ace' in Satan's pack was gloriously trumped by the resurrection. Now all Satan's cards are on the table and he has no more hidden up his sleeve.

Knowledge is power, and Satan kept knowledge of his own activity hidden from mankind, until Jesus flushed him out of his hidden lair. If we carefully study the narrative of Jesus' life and death, and evaluate it by means of biblical truth and personal experience, we shall discover every tactic ever devised by Satan's mind. We now have the knowledge which brings power to recognise and to resist the devil's attacks. There is, therefore, no essential reason why we should ever be taken by surprise in this spiritual warfare – at least in theory. The more we take in both Old Testament and New Testament teaching on the character and work of the devil, and interpret our daily experience in its light, the more easily we shall recognise how and where enemy action is being directed.

THE ENEMY'S TRAITS

Before we look at Paul's references to the devil in this

letter, it is important to note three essential characteristics of our enemy. First of all, he is an imitator. Satan never invented or created anything; he is himself a created being who has rebelled against the Creator. He can imitate the creative work of God with convincing copies: the most dangerous cults and sects are those closest to the Christian gospel. As an imitator, he is also constantly copying himself. He has nothing new to reveal to the world. He spends his time revamping old material. Once we have discerned the way he operates in a particular situation, we can be sure he will try the same trick again. That is one way in which he is so completely the reverse of God, who is always creative, always new, always fresh.

Satan is also a deceiver. The truth is in God and revealed by God: all Satan can do with it is to warp it, misreport it, or contradict it. The narrative in Genesis 3 of his encounter with Adam and Eve illustrates all three tendencies. Whenever something less than the truth is accepted in a Christian's life, or in the life of a church, the deceiver has won a victory.

Satan is also a destroyer: it is this characteristic which controls all he does. He wants ultimately to destroy everything and everyone created by God. Jesus exposed this fundamental facet of the devil's character when he affirmed: 'You are of your father the devil, and your will is to do your father's desires. He was a murderer from the beginning, and has nothing to do with the truth, because there is no truth in him. When he lies, he speaks according to his own nature, for he is a liar and the father of lies' (John 8: 44).

The occasions in 2 Corinthians when Paul refers to the devil point to several ways in which he operates in his basic character as an imitator, a deceiver and a destroyer. Some of these situations we have examined already or shall examine in subsequent chapters: but it will be helpful to consider the overall panorama presented by each in turn.

Unresolved relationships (2 Cor. 2: 10–11). The issue is forgiveness, the forgiveness by Paul and the Corinthians of a particular individual who had thrown off control. Discipline had been administered. Repentance had resulted. Restoration was now being established – 'to keep Satan from gaining the advantage over us'. He will always try to pressurise Christians, but there is no need ever to let him gain the upper hand. One of the major ways he establishes effective control in a local church is when a repentant sinner is not unconditionally welcomed back into the fellowship.

I can think of one particular situation where the painful truth of Paul's remarks has been amply illustrated. A Christian had gone over the top in a particular relationship, leading to deep hurt in the person sinned against – although it was never an open-and-shut case in terms of personal responsibility resting with only one party. After considerable trauma in negotiation and confrontation, this Christian received a measure of disciplining and reached a place of repentance. This was never accepted by the other person as adequate, because it was felt strongly that there needed to be demonstrable and consistent evidence of change – evidence which only the injured party felt able to monitor. Because the injury was so deep, everyone still awaits unconditional reconciliation. In the meantime, Satan has had quite a field day in the fellowship of believers, and especially in the personal life of the injured party.

I believe it is easy enough to find good human reasons for the inability of this person to reach a place of offering forgiveness and of finding reconciliation. My major point is this: God's forgiveness of us and reconciliation with us does not lay down conditions or set periods of probation. That is the love which is to determine our relationships with one another in his family. When it does not do so, Satan has won an advantage. He has set himself the task of fouling up relationships. He started off that way in the

Garden of Eden, driving a wedge between Adam and Eve, so that each blamed the other for the misery they brought upon themselves by their disobedience. Wherever sin remains unrepented and unforgiven, whenever Christians remain unreconciled, there the devil is at work.

Unenlightened thinking (2 Cor. 4: 3, 4). Unbelievers are prevented from experiencing the light of the gospel by the direct activity of 'the god of this world'. He puts a veil over people's thinking, and that veil produces blindness. This blindness prevents people seeing who Jesus is and what he has done. I find I constantly have to remind myself of this fact in personal encounter with those who have a low estimate of Jesus, and a persistent misunderstanding of his mission and salvation. It is *not* simply – or fundamentally – a matter of more information, discussion and time. It is not even a matter only of incarnating the love of Jesus in a convincing and winning manner. It is a matter of recognising the spiritual blindness caused by a spiritual foe, and using spiritual weapons to bring spiritual sight.

Paul prays to this end for those who have already had their eyes opened to exercise saving faith in Jesus as Lord:

> I do not cease to give thanks for you, remembering you in my prayers, that the God of our Lord Jesus Christ, the Father of glory, may give you a spirit of wisdom and of revelation in the knowledge of him, having the eyes of your hearts enlightened, that you may know what is the hope to which he has called you, what are the riches of his glorious inheritance in the saints, and what is the immeasurable greatness of his power in us who believe, according to the working of his great might which he accomplished in Christ when he raised him from the dead (Eph. 1: 16–20).

Paul's phrase, 'the god of this world', is a deliberate *double entendre*, evoking both the power and the

impotence of the devil. John went so far as to declare that
'the whole world is in the power of the evil one' (1 John 5:
19), but in virtually the same breath proclaims that 'any
one born of God . . . the evil one does not touch' (1 John 5:
18). However inexorable is the impact of truth, it is not
self-evident to those in the grip of this archetypal liar.
However radical the revolution of God's Spirit in the lives
of those who receive Jesus as Lord, a mighty act of
revelation is required – and is continuously required – to
illuminate with truth the minds of believers. We cannot
afford to play down the reality and the seriousness of this
aspect of Christians' spiritual conflict.

Unequal marriages (2 Cor. 6: 15). We have already
considered the application of this passage to relationships
other than marriage.[3] It clearly does have relevance to
marriage and it is crucial to be unambiguous about the
importance the devil attaches to preventing, or snarling
up, full-blooded Christian partnerships. It is probably no
exaggeration to say that he uses all his devices to achieve
disaster in this area. He will imitate the real thing. He will
deceive with half-truths and outright lies. He will destroy
faith, whole-heartedness and obedience to God's will –
and along the way worship will be eroded, peace and joy
will be dissipated, and desire for God will be evaporated.

The chief deception practised by Satan on Christians
contemplating marriage with non-Christians is in con-
ning them into thinking that there will be harmony on
most things, but discord only in one aspect of the
relationship – i.e. the religious. Christian marriage is a
'symphony' (the literal meaning of the word translated
'accord'), which can be played only by those responding to
the same conductor.

Those who fight this truth get tired of and angry with
pastors who proceed to tell story after story of spiritual
disaster in unequal marriages. I know that two Christians
do not necessarily make a successful marriage: but I am

concerned with the quality of our discipleship in terms of obedience to God's word, not with statistics about broken homes or apparent exceptions to the rule. We are playing fast and loose with the Lordship of Jesus when we flirt with the possibility, as Christians, of contracting a marriage with an unbeliever. The surest way, in any context, of letting the devil manipulate our lives is by deliberately disobeying the word of God.

Because there may well be those reading these paragraphs who have gone ahead with such an unequal marriage, let it be said with similar clarity that there is a way back into hope and peace with God. It is the same path as for any rebel – the path of repentance. We shall reap what we have sown, but God is able to take it all and turn it into something worthwhile in his kingdom. The repentance may also pave the way for the unbelieving partner to find faith – a possibility at present blocked by any determination to justify disobedience by our own attempts to convert our partner.

Unrestrained pride (2 Cor. 10: 3-6). Although the devil is not explicitly mentioned in these verses, the language of spiritual warfare indicates Paul's awareness of the enemy's presence and methods. He has been accused of operating in Christian ministry 'according to the flesh' (2 Cor. 1: 12, 17 AV) – an accusation frequently levelled at him by his detractors.[4] For any Christian, let alone an apostle, to approach Christian service and witness with fleshly, human or worldly resources denotes not merely downright folly, but intense pride.

'Men fortify themselves against God: they try to find impregnable positions in which they may defy him and live their own life. Human nature, when God is announced to speak, instinctively puts itself on its guard; and you cannot pass that guard with weapons furnished by the flesh.'[5]

Paul's retort to his detractors is, therefore, very pungent:

For though we live in the world we are not carrying on a
worldly war, for the weapons of our warfare are not
worldly but have divine power to destroy strongholds,
We destroy arguments and every proud obstacle to the
knowledge of God, and take every thought captive to
obey Christ, being ready to punish every disobedience . . .

God resists the proud, and the inner nature of Satan is
his pride. It was for his pride that he himself was punished
by God. In a highly dramatic passage in Isaiah, we are told
that God 'has a day against all that is proud and lofty'
towards his sovereign rule in people's lives (Isa. 2: 5–22).
In that passage three particular arenas for Satan's proud
activity are mentioned – mediumship, materialism and
militarism. It is only the deception of Satan which fools
anyone into believing that any of these things is anything
but anathema to God. Each has human – and Satanic –
pride as its root. Mediumship provides an imitation of
God's living relationship with his people. Materialism is
the most common deception which the devil foists on men
and women, based on the lie that material possessions
bring happiness. Militarism is the final destructive
weapon that Satan has manufactured, especially in a
nuclear age.

The unrestrained pride of modern man has blinded
many professing Christians into believing that this
ungodly trinity – in part or in whole – can in some sense go
hand in hand with obedient discipleship. There is no such
thing as Christian spiritualism. God does not regard the
Western world's love of things as anything but idolatry.
The build-up of nuclear and conventional weaponry does
not meet with divine approval because it is directed
against a Marxist superpower: where in the Bible does it
ever state – or even hint – that God loves the people of the
'free world' more than communists? It is human pride
which thinks that, let alone attempts to give divine
sanction to militarism.

'Pride hates equally the thought of absolute indebtedness to God and the thought of standing on the same level with others in God's sight. This pride raises in every part of our nature its protest against the great surrender.'[6] Satan plays on our pride and in so doing talks a lot about God, according to the testimony of the Bible;[7] but that is why he is so dangerous. Pride is dangerous and it is good for us to appreciate its origins.

Undiscriminating tolerance (2 Cor. 11: 2-4, 13-15). Paul was intensely devoted to the spiritual well-being of all those whom he had led to faith in Christ. He was especially jealous for the Corinthian Christians – 'I feel a divine jealousy for you, for I betrothed you ... as a pure bride to her one husband.' As we have seen, he wanted them to remain open to God, to himself, and to one another – to retain 'a sincere and pure devotion to Christ.'

In his concern for the comparatively immature Christians at Corinth, Paul warns them against being gullible about those who preach 'another Jesus ... a different spirit ... a different gospel'. He sees the scheming of such people as on a par with and taking its cue from Satan's original luring of Eve away from her trusting obedience to God. The word translated 'cunning' in 11: 3 has the connotation of doing anything to pervert simple faith in God. Satan will stop at nothing to undermine young disciples. He fought hard to prevent the veil being stripped from their minds: he now bends his mind to the purpose of getting them into cul-de-sacs and byways.

There is a particular lure in complex and contemporary wisdom. Any thinking person finds the gospel's exclusive claims extremely hard to accept, especially when it requires proper defence before sophisticated or crude critics. It is very tempting to sit rather lightly to the Jesus of the New Testament, to accept the expurgations which some modern theologians make, and to come up with a Jesus who does not talk about hell, perform miracles, or literally rise from the dead. It is also alluring to speak in terms of a universal spirit of goodness in every person, rather than the Holy Spirit whom the world neither knows nor can receive (John 14: 16–17). When another Jesus and a different spirit have been taken on board, the message which sounds forth is bound to be another gospel, totally different from the good news of salvation through Jesus Christ. The mighty river of Christian revelation is then left to roll on almost unvisited, while erstwhile believers sail aimlessly on the vast 'sea of faith'.

Such undiscriminating tolerance, so popular in today's syncretistic atmosphere, is a feature of Satanic activity. What is at stake is not so much the exposure of truth to falsehood (we need never fear that), but the personal allegiance in young believers to Jesus as Lord. If those who so debunk a straightforward love for Christ could demonstrate that their way leads to more valid expressions of Christian discipleship and to clearer demonstrations of the Lordship of Jesus, then it would be easier to treat them as serious Christians. As it is, there seems little commitment to evangelism and little desire to glorify Jesus Christ. Until the evidence begins to point in a God-ward direction, it is legitimate to see in their tactics a symptom of Satan's cunning.

A few verses later, Paul refers to the devil as a master of disguises, who masquerades as 'an angel of light'. He rarely comes to us as a roaring lion,[8] because we should have no difficulty recognising him and our helplessness would immediately drive us back on the power of Christ. No, the devil's most dangerous ploy is to convince us by a façade of pseudo-goodness. As Denney explains, 'evil could never tempt us if we saw it simply as it is; disguise is essential to its power.'[9]

* * *

Two final points can act as summary of this theme, one from Paul's last specific mention of Satan (2 Cor. 12: 7), the other from the passages where he does *not* mention him.

Paul's final reference to Satan perfectly crystallises his overall perspective. He refers to 'a thorn in the flesh', the identity of which remains obscure in spite of over thirty-five suggestions over the centuries. This painful impediment, which so underlined the apostle's weakness, was 'given' to him – Paul clearly means, given by God. But he also calls it 'a messenger of Satan'. Here we touch again one of the supreme paradoxes of the New Testament: the nagging impediment sent by Satan was a gift of God.[10]

But perhaps the most striking fact about Paul's attitude to Satan is that he does *not* mention him in passages where, if he had thought and taught like many Christians today, we should have anticipated it most frequently. I refer to the four passages where he is most articulate about the pressures and the suffering he has faced in his Christian experience. These are 2 Cor. 1: 3–11; 4: 7–5: 10; 6: 3–10 and 11: 23–33. In them there is no mention at all of Satanic intervention or cause. If Paul was 'not ignorant of his designs', these silences are as eloquent and instructive as the references we have just examined. We need to develop a similar caution, as well as a similar clarity, in talking about the devil and all his works.

14

SECTARIANISM

The defaulting soldier who reckons everyone else is out of step is proverbial. There is a streak in human nature which makes us all convinced we are right and others are wrong. From one perspective the history of the Christian Church is the story of another group or another individual thinking their way is right – and opting out of the mainstream to found yet another congregation, which probably becomes a denomination or disappears with the death or demise of its leader. A sad result of such a tendency is seen, for example, in over 2,000 different (and unconnected) Pentecostal congregations in one African city alone. In many parts of the world today the most striking fact about the Christian Church is its subdivision into more and more groups – a phenomenon which obscures and even threatens to nullify the numerical increase in the Church.

This sectarian spirit is so pervasive that we need to examine its characteristics. Not one of us is innocent of sectarianism, even the most charitable and comprehensive Christian. Even those most committed to ecumenism take up a very dismissive stance towards those who are opposed to ecumenism. We all disenfranchise one another, given the necessary provocation and half a chance. As Denney puts it, 'Human nature loves a monopoly ... We are all too

ready to unchurch, or unchristianise, others.'[1] I am sure,
for example, that sensitive souls can easily find marks of
sectarianism in this book.

IS PAUL ENTIRELY GUILTLESS?

I am not entirely sure that Paul is himself free of it in the
last part of 2 Corinthians, chapters 10–13, in which he
admits he has been provoked into untypical and foolish
statements.[2] He certainly seems to end up accusing his
detractors at Corinth of being something far more terrible
than we initially suspected. The phrases, 'false apostles,
deceitful workmen, disguising themselves as apostles of
Christ' (11: 13) may sound harsh to us, but make sense in
terms of Paul's distinctive apostleship and its importance
for Christian truth. But when he goes on to call them
servants of Satan, whose 'end will correspond to their
deeds' (11: 15) there is reason to question his emotional
objectivity. I do not doubt for one moment the crucial
importance of safeguarding, particularly young, believers
from falsehood and error. No doubt, as we saw in the last
chapter, Satan specialises in lies and deceit. Nevertheless,
there is insufficient evidence in the available texts of the
Corinthian correspondence to substantiate the unconditional condemnation Paul eventually pronounces on his
opponents.

Having made this tentative rider about Paul's own
impartiality vis-à-vis the sectarians at Corinth, we still
find a very shrewd analysis of the sectarian spirit in these
last four chapters of the letter. There seem to be at least ten
characteristics: accusing others of operating 'in the flesh';
writing off the ministry of others; mutual rivalry; pride in
visible results; claiming credit ourselves for the work of
others; emphasis on fine speaking; discovery of new truth;
insistence that others support us financially; ambitious
and authoritarian leadership; attaching overriding im-

portance to visions and revelations. Because none of us is free from sectarianism, we shall all be challenged by Paul's analysis.

Accusing others of operating in the flesh. Five times in this letter Paul uses the phrase 'according to the flesh'. The English translations obscure the refrain, which was clearly the nub of the dismissive verdict on Paul and his ministry at Corinth made by his detractors. These five occasions suggest that Paul was thus accused in terms of his daily behaviour (2 Cor. 1: 12), his decision-making (1: 17), his treatment of people (5: 16), his evangelistic ministry (10: 2), and his priorities in ministry (11: 18). As Plummer comments, 'His opponents attributed to him unspiritual and worldly motives and conduct; that he was capricious and shuffling, verbose and vain-glorious, at once a coward and a bully.'[3]

This accusation inevitably touched Paul on the raw. His opponents were taking a fundamental Christian truth, expounded by the apostle himself with immense vigour and insight, and hurling it back in his face: 'You talk about the flesh and the spirit, the menace of one and the importance of the other – and all the time you are operating according to the flesh yourself.' The net result of these barbed words can be detected in Paul's rueful comment later on: 'if I come again I will not spare them – since you desire proof that Christ is speaking in me' (13: 2–3). It is clear from this remark that Paul's ministry at Corinth was being described as, not merely not in the Spirit, but lacking any real Christ-content. However much he talked *about* Christ, it was being said, there was no evidence at all that Christ was speaking in and through him.

SUPER-SPIRITUAL

This super-spiritual accusation is very common. I have

frequently found such language and similar attitudes, not just in the congregations where I have served but in many which I have visited. On home ground the conversation tends to be kept from those in leadership, and is confined to those who 'see things the way we do' – there is, apparently, not enough prayer, no proper listening to God, either too much or too little loyalty to ecclesiastical authority, not enough support of the 'right' ideas/people/priorities. The list could be extended lengthily.

When I travel, the situation is similar but takes on subtly different dynamics. When a visiting speaker comes to an area or a congregation, the advertised subject tends to be of appeal to those who take everything fairly seriously. My main theme when travelling has been the life of the local church – a fairly large subject, but topical and relevant for most Christians. It is as certain as it can be that, early on in the proceedings, I shall be button-holed by an earnest group of people who are all 'really concerned about the Rector'. What emerges is a catalogue of criticisms about his 'unspiritual' approach to ministry. The recitative invariably is concluded by an aria about hiving off to form a fellowship of people who 'really mean business with the Lord'.

Now it is all too easy, as I can painfully testify, to operate in the flesh, not in the Spirit. But there is an ugly sectarianism in those who constantly accuse everyone else, especially those carrying pastoral responsibility, of worldly and unspiritual behaviour. This is particularly true when it is done in a spirit of criticism behind another's back, instead of in a spirit of love face to face. It is also noticeable that frequently such accusations of unspirituality tend to come from those who have already distanced themselves from the heart of the local fellowship – and in some cases they were never in at the heart, but have brought their critical spirit with them from another rejected church.

Writing off the ministry of others. This is the inevitable result of resorting to the tactics just described. Those of a sectarian spirit, I think unconsciously, do dismiss the ministry of Christians in this way. It is fairly obvious that Paul was thus written off by the intruders at Corinth. He actually quotes one of their remarks, ' "His letters are weighty and strong, but his bodily presence is weak, and his speech is of no account" ' (2 Cor. 10: 10).

Now that is a fairly swingeing comment, effectively discounting everything he had taught at Corinth. In so doing, they also virtually obliterated the value of his correspondence with the Corinthians, by impugning its integrity. When we pause to recall that Paul founded the church at Corinth and that this was the first generation of the Christian Church, we can appreciate precisely how sectarian his opponents had become. They wanted to start all over again, with themselves in charge. I am personally not surprised that these people got under Paul's skin so successfully.

NOT LISTENING TO GOD

I still remember with considerable pain the time when my own ministry was thus written off by people I had scarcely met. I was away on leave at the time, with the pastoral care of the congregation in the hands of a team of laymen but with another recently ordained person due to join us (he arrived before I returned from leave). While I was away, one member of the pastoral team became strongly influenced by the people I mentioned. Soon after I returned, he suddenly burst out with a tirade against my ministry, writing it off as unspiritual because I was not listening properly to God.

In addition, I discovered much later that my newly-ordained colleague had been in conversation with the same people, very soon after his arrival in the parish but just before my return. They were understandably discussing me and my ministry. When he passed the comment, 'I understand David has a fine teaching ministry,' the reaction came back, 'We're not so sure about that' – a low-key, but fairly dismissive remark, especially in that particular context. Only loyalty, and a resolute refusal to be prematurely prejudiced, kept my colleague from jumping to all kinds of conclusions.

I have found, over the years, that this aspect of sectarianism has been most prevalent among those who have not experienced the stresses and strains of pastoral responsibility for a congregation. To such people the issues are apparently very clear and uncomplicated. They have probably been involved in Christian work in other ways which are equally important, but never in the complex, interpersonal realities of local church life, as pastors entrusted with the care of God's people as a whole.

Paul's work among the Corinthians had been so completely dismissed by such detractors, that he even had to remind the Christians of what had happened among them under his ministry: 'I was not at all inferior to these superlative apostles, even though I am nothing. The signs of a true apostle were performed among you in all patience, with signs and wonders and mighty works' (2 Cor. 12: 11-12).

The Corinthians had been so taken in by Paul's opponents that they had concluded he was a failure, not merely as an apostle and ambassador for Christ, but as a Christian. In fact, it seems that they were doubting even if he was a Christian at all. This amazing conclusion is mentioned when Paul urges them to examine themselves 'to see whether you are holding to your faith.' They had forgotten the basics: 'Test yourselves. Do you not realise that Jesus Christ is in you? – unless indeed you fail to meet the test! I hope you will find out that we have not failed' (13: 5-6). When the ministry and the discipleship of the apostle Paul can be thus impugned, we can see the seriousness of sectarianism.

Mutual rivalry. At first glance, it is surprising to find those imbued with the sectarian spirit engaged in rivalry and competitiveness among one another. Further consideration brings a ready explanation: if their initial and underlying approach to Christian work consists of favourable comparisons between their own ministry and that of others, such attitudes will not disappear once they have established a foothold. It is, therefore, to be expected that Paul comments on them in these revealing words: 'But when they measure themselves by one another, and compare themselves with one another, they are without understanding' (2 Cor. 10: 12).

Paul's comments point to a double-sided mutual comparison. One side normally precedes the other in becoming obvious, but the one leads as surely to the other as night leads to day. First, such people have mutually-agreed criteria of spirituality: if you meet these, you are one of them; if you excel in them, you are highly esteemed. Denney writes: 'They constitute a religious coterie, a sort of clique or ring in the church, ignoring all but themselves, making themselves the only standard of what is Christian.'[4] Examples of this are so common that they scarcely need explaining: charismatics against non-charismatics, evangelicals against non-evangelicals, radicals against non-radicals. Anglo-Catholics against non-Anglo-Catholics, ecumenists against non-ecumenists. It is, indeed, symptomatic of the sectarian spirit than those it castigates are invariably labelled 'not . . .' or 'non . . .'.

'They measure themselves by one another,' says Paul, and the mentality of sectarianism can never brook the outsiders' criticism. 'Others do not understand us; they are not on the same wavelength; some day they will see the light' – these are the watchwords of modern, as of ancient, gnostics who believe that they, and only they, have the truth.

But if we start measuring ourselves purely by one another, very soon a competitive and judgmental attitude will emerge within our close fellowship. The very criteria which guarantee membership also promote rivalry and witch-hunts. In such an atmosphere it is imperative to retain one's credibility. What pervades it is a constant comparing by one with another. The result? Eventually, a few will break off from the group to form another clique of like-minded people. And so the sectarian spirit marches on and Jesus suffers once again as his body is further torn asunder.

It would be easy to multiply examples of this sectarianism from recent and current Church life. Little would be gained by such a list. If we begin to detect and to deal with any marks of competitiveness in our own attitudes, especially in the church to which we belong, we shall have gained much.

Pride in visible results. We all know the powerful temptation to parade before others the results of our ministry. The sectarian spirit feeds off this temptation. It is plain from what Paul does *not* say, rather than what he does say, that his opponents at Corinth made a great noise about their achievements. He is himself eventually lured into making several claims of his own – the theme of boasting is pervasive in this letter, but especially in the last four chapters.[5]

Unlike his detractors, Paul regards certain boasting as off-limits. He found no need to pile up the evidence for his success, for his own benefit or for the benefit of his 'public'. He was certainly not intending to boast 'in other men's labours' (2 Cor. 10: 15). When he does eventually start to boast, he begins with a few credit-lines (Hebrews, Israelites, descendants of Abraham, servants of Christ (11: 22–3)), but he soon moves into 'the things that show my weakness' (11: 23–30).

The sectarian spirit loves statistics and success stories. It needs to have them publicised and written up – and the Christian public unfortunately seems to enjoy the accounts. At bottom, the reason for this concentration on success is self-justification: if we hive off from the existing Church, either organisationally or simply by keeping ourselves to ourselves, we must justify the action by the results – however much we believe and declare initially that the new departure or the accepted policy of our church is a matter of obedience to the Spirit of God, of the Word of God, or both.

The quotation Paul gives from Jeremiah is pungent and challenging: 'Let him who boasts boast of the Lord.'[6] The fuller context in Jeremiah is equally relevant: we are urged not to boast in our wisdom, might or riches. A modern paraphrase might well run: 'Do not boast about your monopoly of the truth, the size of your congregation, or the amount you give away to missionary work; boast in the Lord who practises steadfast love, justice and right-eousness in the earth.' Those last three priorities are the ones God looks for in his Church.

Taking the credit for the work of other Christians. It seems that Paul was riled most of all by the way the people at Corinth claimed the credit for what he had spent himself unstintingly bringing into reality. They had done nothing to initiate or build the church at Corinth. They had jauntily ridden in on the back of Paul's toil and tears, making vast capital out of the temporary coolness in the apostle's relationship with the church in the city. They saw the church at Corinth as their own field of operation and let everyone else know they were in charge. This is plain from Paul's remarks: 'We do not boast beyond limit, in other men's labours; but our hope is that as your faith increases, our field among you may be greatly enlarged, so that we may preach the gospel in lands beyond you, without boasting of work already done in another's field' (2 Cor. 10: 15–16).

Denney's comments on these verses illustrate the attitude of Paul's opponents and show the way out of such sectarianism. 'They did not propagate the Gospel,' he writes, 'with apostolic enthusiasm among the heathen; they waited till Paul had done the hard preliminary work, and formed Christian congregations everywhere, and then they slunk into them, talking as if these churches were their work... The show is divine, but the reality is diabolical.'[7] Denney's answer to this is clear: 'The safeguard of the soul against this base spirit is an interest like Paul's in the Christianising of those who do not know Christ at all.'[8]

I am excited when I hear of new churches springing up in areas where there is no witness to Christ. There are increasing numbers of such churches. I am sad, however, to hear of many situations where yet another church is formed, usually of malcontents, in areas where there is abundant Christian testimony. In such cases I am reluctant to accuse people of sectarianism, but the signs are not always promising – especially if there is no heart for evangelism.

The desire to win unbelievers to Christ as Lord is an essential and authentic mark of the Church. When Christians form a fellowship of like-minded people where Paul's missionary zeal is absent, that is sectarianism, especially when it goes hand in glove with gaining new members from the disaffected attenders of existing congregations. That habit is the established tactic of cults like the Mormons, Jehovah's Witnesses and Moonies.

Emphasis on fine speaking. The personality cult has become an extremely powerful trend in today's media-dominated world. The Church has allowed itself to be heavily conditioned by this trend. We seem to need, even to demand, leadership which is able to articulate the Christian message with charisma, charm and conviction. By this conformity to secular priorities we are encouraging the spirit of sectarianism, which has always majored on the priority of fine speaking.

Paul cannot have been useless as a public speaker. At Lystra he was called Hermes by the locals, because he was the chief speaker and they thought that in Barnabas and Paul '"The gods have come down to us in the likeness of men!"' (Acts 14: 8–13). When he came to Corinth, he deliberately eschewed any temptation to speak with eloquent rhetoric (1 Cor. 2: 1–5). Perhaps he over-reacted. But his detractors at Corinth latched on to any actual or alleged weakness as a speaker, and wrote him off. He simply was not in the top league (2 Cor. 10: 10; 11: 6).

By introducing this emphasis on fine speaking as a touchstone for Christian leadership, these people at Corinth were foisting on the Church a particularly dangerous attitude. Because preaching and teaching are of such importance in the Christian community, it is all too easy to give more attention to those who preach well and teach well. When the limelight falls on these people, a personality cult is encouraged which imperceptibly pushes certain individuals to the front of the stage.

Such is the nature of fallen humanity that individuals, given this publicity and such high profile, slowly come to believe the applause they receive. They then become very difficult to hold down, live with, correct and contain. They often go out on a limb. If they remain linked to one particular church in a denomination, they sit very loose to its overseeing responsibility. They remain in demand as speakers at conferences and big events. They develop a following, through tapes and books as well as through straight public speaking. All these factors encourage the development of a sectarian spirit. The whole syndrome is catastrophically boosted by the electronic church in the USA.

Discovery of new truth. One of the buttresses for the position taken up by a group like Paul's detractors at Corinth is the claim to have rediscovered a long-neglected truth, or even to have found something new. The latter

claim is normally made by those with no knowledge of
Church history, the former by those who have a smattering
of such knowledge.

Paul had to contend with those who were pushing
'another Jesus... a different spirit... a different gospel' (2
Cor. 11: 4). That was his language: no doubt his
opponents came to Corinth with talk of the real Jesus...
what the Holy Spirit is really all about... and a gospel
which has not been perverted by Paul's own hang-ups and
personal agenda. We hear such language frequently today.

This kind of message is constantly a predicament in the
life of local churches. The rediscovery of neglected biblical
truth is a constant necessity, if the Church as a whole is to
be faithful to the gospel. But it is not necessary to take a
freshly-discovered insight and use it as a basis for schism
and separation. In recent years this kind of thing has
happened over matters related to baptism, gifts of the
Spirit, ordination, and church government – all issues on
which there has been more formal and historical
denominationalism in the last 400 years, or less.

Other issues have produced a sectarian spirit, if not
actual division – styles of worship, the place of Israel in
God's purposes, the ordination of women, political
allegiance and convictions, and there are probably several
others. The sheer variety of divisive issues indicates the
danger of the sectarian spirit.

Insistence that others support us financially. This facet of
sectarianism needs some careful explanation, because in
Paul's case this issue was central to his precarious
standing with the Corinthians, once his detractors got to
work on them.

While he was at Corinth Paul steadily refused to accept,
or even to ask for, maintenance from the Corinthians. In
his first letter he made it plain that he could have insisted
on it on several convincing grounds (1 Cor. 9: 3–12). But he
deliberately refrained from claiming his rights to be

looked after materially by those who were indebted to him
for their spiritual life and growth. He refrained, because
he wanted absolutely nothing to come in the way of the
free gift of salvation proclaimed by the gospel. In Paul's
mind he could have seriously prejudiced the impact of his
message, if he had demanded payment for his services.

Now his detractors at Corinth chose to hold this refusal
against him. Real apostles, they insisted, have a right to
maintenance from their converts – if Paul did not exercise
that right, it showed that he actually did not believe he was
an apostle. Therefore he was hoodwinking the Corinthians all the time, coming on strong with them and
insisting on this and that in their discipleship, but
actually not possessing any real authority at all. They
concluded their unpleasant denigration of Paul's motives
and methods by asserting: 'He doesn't really care for you;
in fact, he has been leaning heavily on you all with his
oppressive personality and claims to be an apostle' (2 Cor.
11: 7-11).

Paul's answer to these snide comments is to appeal to
the Corinthians' inner knowledge of his love for them:
'God knows I do [love you] . . . I am ready to come to you.
And I will not be a burden to you, for I seek not what is
yours but you . . . I will most gladly spend and be spent for
your souls' (2 Cor. 11: 11; 12: 14-15). The key phrase seems
to be: 'I seek not what is yours but you.' By implication,
Paul is accusing his accusers of being in Christian
ministry for what they can get out of it. He thinks they are
not at all concerned for the Corinthians, only for what the
Corinthians can give them. In other words, they are
hirelings, not shepherds, and care not a jot for the sheep –
which is not surprising, because the sheep are not theirs
anyway.[9]

The contrast between Paul and his detractors is
complete. He had the right to insist on maintenance by the
Corinthians, but he freely waived it in the interests of the
gospel; they had no right to insist on maintenance because

they were not true shepherds of the flock, but they did insist on it as a right and imposed it on the Corinthians. This kind of insistence is a mark of sectarianism, which turns the freedom of the gospel into rules and regulations. Supporting those who minister God's word and care for the flock is one of the willing responses given freely by a grateful congregation who know the joy of the gospel. But to insist that it is something which *must* be done is to impose a heavy burden. And many such burdens are imposed on God's people, when the sectarian spirit introduces a new legalism into a congregation.

Ambitious and authoritarian leadership. This ingredient is closely linked with the previous one. In a sense, an insistence that church members financially support those in pastoral leadership is just one example of what happens when people work their way into prominence. This is what had happened at Corinth. These people had demonstrably pushed themselves into leadership: they were ambitious men. They wanted to exercise influence in the Church of God. They could not take a humble position and be servants in the household.

Once they had the authority they wanted, they exercised it in the same spirit. Paul describes it in the following words: 'For you bear it if a man makes slaves of you, or preys upon you, or takes advantage of you, or puts on airs, or strikes you in the face' (2 Cor. 11: 20). Each phrase vividly illustrates the way authoritarian leadership can operate.

The first phrase is particularly powerful, because it describes the kind of leadership which makes slaves of people, by binding them irretrievably to themselves, making them dependent upon their leadership and demanding unquestioning obedience. The contrast with Paul's understanding of leadership is complete: he saw himself as the slave of those in his care, ready to spend and be spent in their service.

The second phrase, 'preys', reiterates the financial motives of the Corinthian self-appointees. Anyone with some experience in pastoral ministry knows how ready some people are to give generously to support the ministry. This can be so easily abused or, even worse, turned to personal gain. The Corinthians were being soaked by such unscrupulous leaders, of a kind with the scribes whom Jesus castigated for their ostentation and greed: 'Beware of the scribes, who like to go about in long robes, and love salutations in the market places and the best seats in the synagogues and the places of honour at feasts, who devour widows' houses and for a pretence make long prayers' (Luke 20: 46-7).

This description of the scribes is an accurate commentary on Paul's next two phrases, 'takes advantage' and 'puts on airs'. The first word is used of catching fish and stresses the attitude to leadership which treats people as objects rather than persons. The second lays bare any tendency to think of ourselves as important because we are in a position of leadership.

Finally, Paul refers to those who treat Christians like dirt, walking all over them in the name of assumed God-given authority. In his Pastoral epistles, Paul warns against appointing to leadership those given to violence.[10] Physical violence is one temptation, but there are other kinds of violence which are as frighteningly un-Christian as a literal blow in the face: for example, threats of excommunication or of divine punishment if the leadership line is not followed.

Such ambitious and authoritarian leadership is inevitably evidenced in sectarian circles, because the checks and balances of the wider fellowship of the Church have been deliberately cast aside. It is a constant danger in any church and in anyone called to exercise leadership in the Church. Paul's own positive example shines out all the more brightly: 'our authority... the Lord gave for building you up and not for destroying you' (2 Cor. 10: 8) –

a conviction he repeats virtually at the end of the letter (13: 10).

Attaching overriding significance to visions and revelations. There seems little point in Paul's decision to 'go on to visions and revelations of the Lord' (2 Cor. 12: 1), unless these were regarded to be of great importance by his detractors at Corinth. They boasted about their experiences of this kind and, although 'there is nothing to be gained by it', Paul is forced to indulge in the same boasting.

He then describes one particular experience in deliberately objective language – not only to avoid any concentration on his own significance in it, but to prove to everyone concerned that he is no stranger to mystical and indescribable experiences of God. He is agnostic about the details of what happened – 'whether in the body or out of the body I do not know, God knows' (12: 2, 3), a point he repeats for emphasis – but he insists that it is completely improper for anyone to talk openly about such matters: he had heard 'things that cannot be told, which man may not utter' (12: 4).

Paul mentions that he had an 'abundance of revelations' (12: 7) – the word indicates both their frequency and intensity, as well as their extraordinary nature. They were a common occurrence for him. The particular one he has described took place 'fourteen years ago' (12: 2), and it is natural to assume that this is the first time he has ever referred to it. Paul's reticence is most striking.

The chief lesson in Paul's treatment of the subject is that he does not see his revelations as significantly determinative for his public ministry or for the life of the church at Corinth. On the other hand, he urged the Corinthians in his first letter to make proper room in their worship for anyone to bring, among other things, 'a revelation' (1 Cor. 14: 26). Proper weight is to be given to such a revelation, which seems in Paul's mind to be one of the ways in which

a prophetic message is brought from God to a local church
– 'Let two or three prophets speak, and let the others weigh
what is said. If a revelation is made to another sitting by,
let the first be silent. For you can all prophesy one by one,
so that all may learn and be encouraged (1 Cor. 14: 29–31).

So Paul is soberly reticent and cautious about the wider
value of his own 'revelations', but he encourages the
Church as a whole to expect God to 'unveil' (the literal
meaning of the word) his will by this – among other –
means. Any claims to possess insight into God's will by
this means today must be subjected to at least this much
careful scrutiny.

Otherwise, a sharply sectarian position will soon be
adopted. We have seen that it is of the essence of
sectarianism to place oneself above criticism by a
separatist choice of like-minded companions. Paul will
not make any capital out of his *private* visions and
revelations; he endorses only those submitted to the
gathered Christian community – and these must be
weighed. The strong implication of Paul's words is that
the troublemakers at Corinth were not following this
path. It is likely that they were imposing their own
personal visions and revelations on the church at Corinth,
not brooking any criticism, let alone inviting evaluation
by the body of Christ as a whole. Such behaviour was at
least consistent with their authoritarian style of leadership: but it is lethal in any church.

* * *

These are some of the characteristics of sectarianism. Any
ism begins with trends which become habits, which are
themselves then turned into dogma. If we can detect the
marks of a sectarian spirit, we shall be more likely to nip
this particularly unpleasant disease in the bud. When it is
in full flower, its fruits are vicious – as Paul intimates
towards the end of this soul-baring passage:

For I fear that perhaps I may come and find you not what I wish, and that you may find me not what you wish; that perhaps there may be quarrelling, jealousy, anger, selfishness, slander, gossip, conceit, and disorder. I fear that when I come again my God may humble me before you, and I may have to mourn over many of those who sinned before and have not repented of the impurity, immorality, and licentiousness which they have practised (2 Cor. 12: 20-1).

The fruit of sectarianism is plain – 'the works of the flesh'.[11] This is ironic in terms of the accusation levelled at Paul by these Corinthian sectarians that *he* operated according to the flesh. In view of what we have seen in this chapter, however, it is not very surprising.

15

SUCCESS AND FAILURE

The title of this chapter is in many ways misleading, because the modern concepts of success and failure are virtually unknown in the New Testament. Certainly Paul never writes about being a success or succeeding in his ministry. In the last chapter of this letter he does express the hope that the Corinthians 'will find out that we have not failed' (2 Cor. 13: 6). But closer investigation shows that he is using the word 'fail' in a different – or at least specialised – sense. He has just urged the Corinthians to examine carefully 'to see whether you are holding to your faith', recognising the fact that 'Jesus Christ is in you' (13: 5). It is these two basic realities of being a Christian that Paul is highlighting. He trusts that the Corinthians will not fail this elementary test, and he hopes that he can establish the fact that he has not failed it either.

In fact, Paul's concern is far more for the spiritual well-being of the Corinthians than for his ability to pass any tests imposed by the Corinthians or anyone else: 'What we pray for is your improvement' (13: 9). So success and failure of any kind do not feature in Paul's vocabulary. And yet much of the letter in front of us is a radical re-interpretation of what Paul has discovered about God's ideas of success and failure. This is epitomised in the classic description of his 'thorn in the flesh' (12: 7–10), a cameo of Paul's life which enshrines much of the overall teaching of the whole letter.

The first point to notice is that Paul links his thorn in the flesh directly with the visions and revelations of the Lord which he has just described. The suffering and the glory go together in Christian experience, both in the humdrum of everyday discipleship and in the more intense experiences of both blessing and pain. But Paul does not simply comment on the way the two realities are linked: he explains that, in his case at least, there was a specific purpose in God's mind in giving a thorn in the flesh to Paul in the midst of 'abundance of revelations'. This purpose was 'to keep me from being too elated' – a phrase he repeats at the end of the same sentence (12: 7).

TO KEEP HIM HUMBLE

We have previously remarked on the way God resists the proud. Paul could see that unrelieved special blessings, especially through visions and revelations, would have made him puffed up. He, at any rate, needed the painful experience of his 'thorn in the flesh' to keep him properly humble before God. Seeing its value, if not necessity, for his own spiritual growth, did not make it any less unpleasant. Paul wanted to be rid of it. On three occasions he pleaded with God to remove this thorn. Each time he received the same answer: '"My grace is sufficient for you"' (12: 9).

The thorn in the flesh emphasised Paul's vulnerability and need for God's daily grace. That is the basis of Christian discipleship and the essence of Christian growth. It is no accident that we do not know what precisely this thorn in the flesh was. The fact that its identity remains unclear enables us to concentrate on the principle: what matters to God is not our health and our happiness, but our being made like Jesus – and that takes place gradually as we experience more and more of the grace of God.

SIMPLISTIC EQUATIONS

I am aware, from personal and pastoral experience, that it is not easy to live with any simplistic equation of pain and suffering with divine discipline and restraints on our pride. It is manifestly true that much individual suffering has no measurable connection with the pride of the person concerned. An obvious example is the immense suffering caused by drought in Africa. Having made this caveat, I still find myself wondering whether we see our human pride in the light in which God sees it. Does anyone have proper insight into the pervasive way this original sin has eaten into the human heart?

Denney writes: 'The greatest spiritual experiences are incommunicable; even the best men are in danger of elation and pride; and the tendency of these sins is immensely strong, and can only be restrained by constant pressure; pain, though one day to be abolished, is a means of discipline actually used by God.'[1]

I hope I am not being casuistic in drawing a distinction between, on the one hand, seeing causal links between our pride and our suffering, and on the other hand stressing the importance of the way we react to our suffering – which can be full either of pride or of humble trust. Paul does not say that he was given his thorn in the flesh *because* he was being proud, but to *prevent* him from becoming proud. We are, on this basis, justified in creatively seeing suffering as an opportunity to prove the faithfulness of God. It is very possible to see it as the exact opposite – as a demonstration of the unfaithfulness and unfairness of God, with the result that we become bitter and depressed.

Sometimes we react to suffering with resignation,

seeing it as something to be endured – until the morning comes and we are out of the darkness once again. This also is sub-Christian. Paul's example urges us to talk honestly and openly with the Lord about the way we feel, and to be ready for fresh experiences of his grace and power in the midst of everything. That is very different from mere resignation and endurance, which can easily be a subtle form of pride in our inner ability to cope with pressure.

Paul has thus brought us back to the fundamental paradox of authentically Christian experience, as both Jesus and his disciples in every generation have known it: 'when I am weak, then I am strong' (2 Cor. 12: 10). 'Paul withdrew his claim on life for power, predominance and conspicuous success. He was reconciled to experience.'[2] Paul is implicitly urging us to face the realities of our experience honestly and to trust God with them.

As it is said of Jesus: 'But we see Jesus, who for a little while was made lower than the angels, crowned with glory and honour because of the suffering of death, so that by the grace of God he might taste death for every one' (Heb. 2: 9). If we thus allow ourselves to taste our weakness in suffering and apparent failure, we shall know more of the power and the glory of God.

THE POWER AND THE GLORY

The story is told of a little boy who was taken to 'big church' and stayed through the whole service for the first time. The service was from the Book of Common Prayer, in which the Lord's Prayer is said twice, once in full and the second time with the last phrases omitted. The boy confidently joined in the first time; he was delighted to know that part of the script. Imagine his joy when it came round again: this time he joined in with even more fervour, so fervently that he carried on loudly with 'Thine is the kingdom, the power and the glory ...' in the midst of a very pregnant and – to his parents – embarrassing silence. When they all got back home, the father asked his son: 'Why do you think they didn't go on to the power and the glory?' The boy replied: 'Perhaps they don't know anything about the power and the glory.'

Nobody would pretend that it is easy to embrace suffering in the way that Paul is exemplifying. He bears testimony to his own inner and protracted struggle. But he came to know the power of Christ in a way hitherto unsuspected: 'When our weakness makes us incapable of doing anything, God's grace gets full scope to work.'³ Paul reached the point where he was glad to boast of his weaknesses, so that 'the power of Christ may rest upon me' (2 Cor. 12: 9). His Corinthian detractors boasted of their successes and achievements, of their strength and their authority. Paul had been drawn into beginning some low-key boasting in similar vein; but now the wheel has come full circle and he is able to declare: 'For the sake of Christ, then, I am content with weaknesses, insults, hardships, persecutions, and calamities' (12: 10).

TRUE CONTENTMENT

So Paul rests his case, not so much in convincing argument as in his personal discovery of true contentment. He boasts about the things which stress his weakness, not because he sees them as good in themselves nor because he is glorying in being weak, but because such experience of weakness provides the only convincing arena for demonstrating God's power and glory. 'He [Jesus] is not weak in dealing with you, but is powerful in you. For he was crucified in weakness, but lives by the power of God. For we are weak in him, but in dealing with you we shall live with him by the power of God' (2 Cor. 13: 3-4).

I think it is essential at this point to draw a proper distinction between the risen and reigning Lord Jesus and the individual Christian in whom he lives through his Spirit. It often seems to be suggested that the two become merged in a person truly filled with the Spirit, with the result that Christians can be demonstrably powerful for God. This seems a very dangerous half-truth. Paul says very carefully that Jesus is the one who is powerful *in* the Christians at Corinth. The message of 2 Corinthians is that this can be seen by others *only* as Christians embrace those experiences and life-situations which emphasise our own weakness.

The conclusion of the matter is this: in God's eyes, we are on the way to success when we find contentment and advantage in tasting our weakness; we fail when we run away from situations in which he intends us to experience our weakness and his grace. The way of Jesus is along the path of suffering. The glory of God shines on the path and shines out from those walking along the path. The glory of God in all its fullness awaits us at the end of the road.

NOTES

INTRODUCTION

1 I have discovered that the whole series has been reprinted in six volumes in the USA and costs over $200. Even Denney is not worth that!
2 Hodder, 1982.

CHAPTER 1

1 *Eminent Victorian Women*, Weidenfeld and Nicolson, 1981, p. 92.
2 C. K. Barrett, *2 Corinthians*, A. & C. Black, ad loc.
3 John Arkwright, 'O Valiant Hearts', *Hymns Ancient and Modern* Revised, No. 584.
4 Cf. Heb. 7: 25.
5 Denney, p. 14.
6 Denney, p. 16.
7 Cf. Matt. 10: 39.
8 Denney, p. 19.
9 Cf. Acts 20: 34.
10 See his farewell speech to the Ephesian elders in Acts 20: 17–34 for evidence.
11 Cf. Acts 19: 30.
12 Denney, p. 21.
13 Barrett, ad loc.

CHAPTER 2

1. This translation accepts the alternative reading of the Greek text, which has the word *Haploteti*.
2. Cf. chaps. 10-13.
3. Cf. 2 Cor. 10: 9-11.
4. Quoted in the *Sunday Telegraph*, 2 September 1984.
5. Cf. 2 Cor. 1: 17-22.
6. Denney, p. 43.
7. Denney, p. 46.
8. *The Times*, 24 August 1984.

CHAPTER 3

1. See, for example, his book, *Christian Counselling*, Word, 1980.
2. See, for example, his book, *Competent to Counsel*, Presbyterian and Reformed Press, 1970.
3. Cf. Exod. 3: 13ff.
4. Cf. Heb. 12: 2.
5. NB. Peter's reference to both the sufferings and the glory.
6. Cf. John 15: 11; 16: 20-4.
7. Recorded in *Words of Wisdom*, compiled by Michael Daniel and Sally Greenaway, Sidgwick and Jackson, 1982, p. 162.
8. Denney, p. 70.
9. Cf. 1 Cor. 16: 24; 2 Cor. 13: 11, 14; Phil. 1: 18; 1 Thess. 2: 8.
10. See chap. 13.

CHAPTER 4

1. See in particular, Exod. 33: 7-34: 5; 29-35.
2. Denney, p. 89.

3 *Christian Praise*, No. 333.
4 Denney, p. 92.
5 'The Leaden Echo and the Golden Echo', quoted in F. T. Palgrave, *The Golden Treasury*, Oxford University Press, 1964, p. 396.
6 I deal with this theme in chap. 5.
7 Cf. Exod. 17: 2-7 and Num. 20: 6-12.
8 Denney, p. 142.

CHAPTER 5

1 I deal in detail with the subject of repentance in chap. 11.
2 See chap. 8.
3 Quoted in *C. S. Lewis: A Biography*, Green and Hooper, Collins, 1974, p. 293.
4 Harvey Cox, *Religion in the Secular City*, Simon & Schuster, 1984, p. 81.
5 Denney, p. 41.

CHAPTER 6

1 Denney, p. 159.
2 Cf. 1 Cor. 15: 22.
3 Cf. Rom. 8: 21.
4 Denney, p. 163.
5 Cf. Eph. 1: 21.
6 Cf. Acts 18: 3.
7 See, for example, Col. 2: 15.
8 Cf. 1 Cor. 15: 18 and Phil. 1: 23.
9 Denney, p. 186.

CHAPTER 7

1 See, for example, the Authorised Version.

2 See also the Good News Bible.
3 Barrett, ad loc.
4 Denney, p. 212.
5 A. Plummer, I.C.C. on *2 Corinthians*, T. & T. Clark, 1978, p. 188.
6 Denney, p. 221.
7 Denney, p. 218.
8 Denney, p. 213. He also wrote a book on the Atonement entitled *The Christian Doctrine of Reconciliation*, well worth obtaining.
9 Pascal, *Pensees*, Penguin Classics, 1966, p. 168.
10 See Rom. 8: 4–9.
11 Cf. Acts 22: 3, 26: 5; Phil. 3: 5.
12 See Matt. 23: 5–7.
13 See 1 Cor. 14: 14–18.
14 See 1 Cor. 14: 2 and 2 Cor. 12: 1–7.

CHAPTER 8

1 Denney, p. 216.
2 ibid.
3 See Matt. 7: 14.
4 Paul amplifies this in 2 Cor. 11: 23–9.
5 Swete, quoted by Plummer, op. cit., p. 195.
6 Pascal, op. cit., pp. 64, 252–3, 103.

CHAPTER 9

1 An annual convention in the English Lake District with a stress on personal holiness. Begun in the last century, it has counterparts in many different countries.
2 Denney, p. 240.
3 See 1 Cor. 5: 9–13.
4 See 1 Cor. 1: 30.

CHAPTER 10

1 Denney calls this phrase 'the key to all that follows' (p. 250).
2 See the beginning of chap. 6.
3 Plummer, p. 213.
4 See pp. 66–8.

CHAPTER 11

1 See 2 Cor. 7: 14.
2 See chap. 7.
3 Denney, p. 255.
4 Denney, p. 259.
5 See Matt. 18: 15ff.
6 Plummer, p. 216.
7 ibid.

CHAPTER 13

1 See Col. 1: 13.
2 See Eph. 6: 10–18.
3 See chap. 9.
4 See 2 Cor. 1: 12, 17 and 4: 16.
5 Denney, p. 294.
6 Denney, p. 297.
7 See Gen. 3: 1ff. and Matt. 4: 1ff.
8 See 1 Pet. 5: 8.
9 Denney, p. 332.
10 The wider implications of this verse will be examined in context in chap. 15.

CHAPTER 14

1 Denney, p. 303.

2 See, for example, 11: 1, 16, 17, 21, 23 and 12: 1, 11.
3 Plummer, p. 275.
4 Denney, p. 307.
5 See especially 10: 13–18.
6 1 Cor. 1: 31.
7 Denney, p. 309.
8 Denney, p. 310.
9 See John 10: 11–15.
10 See 1 Tim. 3: 3 and Titus 1: 7.
11 See Gal. 5: 19–21.

CHAPTER 15

1 Denney, p. 357.
2 C. H. Dodd, *Bulletin of the John Rylands Library*, 17–18 (1933–4).
3 Denney, p. 356.